Happy Valentines Day!

Love,
Charlene
1977

THE PRO GAME

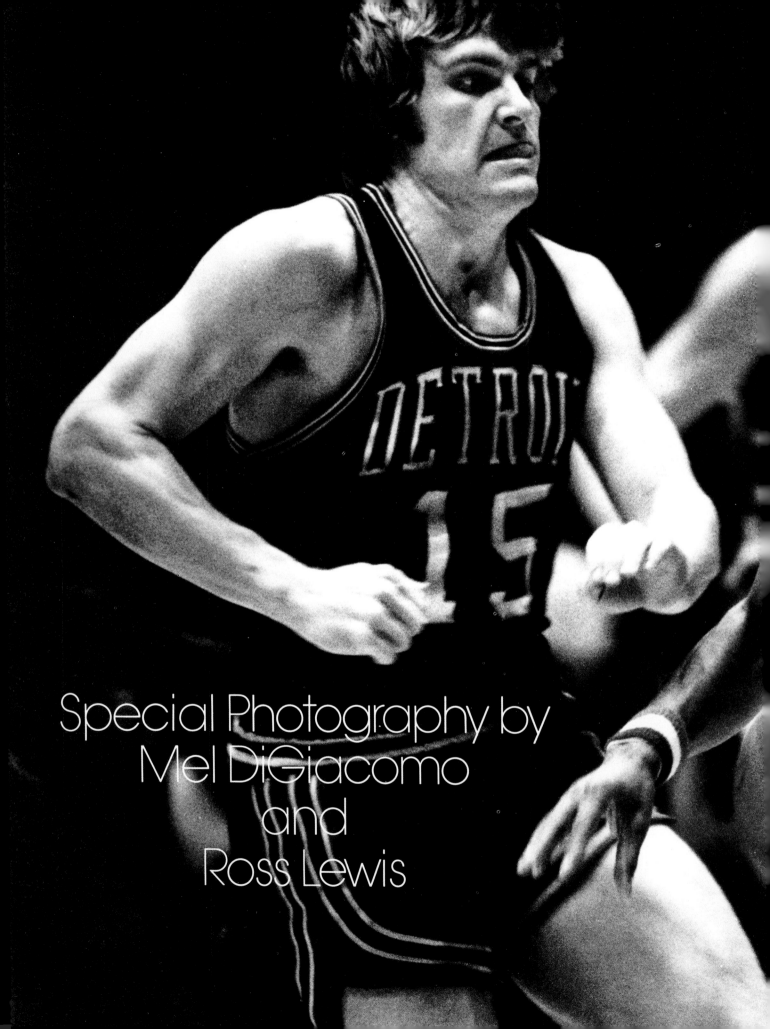

Special Photography by
Mel DiGiacomo
and
Ross Lewis

THE PRO GAME
The World of Professional Basketball
By Bob Ryan

A Rutledge Book
McGraw-Hill Book Company

New York | St. Louis | San Francisco | Toronto

Fred R. Sammis Publisher
John T. Sammis Creative Director
Doris Townsend Editor-in-Chief
Allan Mogel Art Director
Sally Andrews Managing Editor
Jeremy Friedlander Associate Editor
B. G. Murphy Associate Editor
Mimi Koren Associate Editor
Arthur Gubernick Production Consultant
Annemarie Bosch Production Manager
Elyse Shick Art Associate
Eric Marshall Art Associate
Jay Hyams Editorial Assistant

Library of Congress Cataloging in Publication Data
Ryan, Bob
   The pro game.
   1. Basketball. 2. Professionalism in sports.
I. Title.
GV885.R92   796.32'364'0973   75-4500
ISBN 0-07-054357-7

Printed in Italy by Mondadori, Verona.

Game of Precision
Introduction

1

At the core, they are all silly games. Football is 22 men outfitted in knickers, jerseys, cleated shoes, and lethal weapons known as helmets. The intent is to carry an oblong ball across a stripe painted on grass. Between the endless piling up and unpiling of bodies, players perpetrate all sorts of mayhem on one another.

What is hockey but a game in which mostly Canadians skate on an indoor pond, flailing away at a small black rubber disc—as well as at each other—in hopes of knocking the disc into a net?

Golfers walk across acres of countryside attacking a small white ball with long sticks, some wooden at the bottom, others metallic. It is perhaps the only game in which men and women who hit a ball well must chase it themselves.

Who adequately can describe baseball? In this game, balls are thrown, hit, and caught at irregular intervals. Men advance 90 feet at a time around the perimeter of a square, their destination being the same as their starting point. They, too, wear absurdly ugly uniforms consisting of knickers and a top, with billed caps that they wouldn't dream of wearing anywhere else perched on their heads.

Then there is basketball, in which semi-undressed men attempt to throw a ball through a ring suspended 10 feet above the ground. Because the game involves an elevated goal, height is thought to be of paramount importance. "The game is for goons," the critics say, and move on.

Since the game of basketball was devised quite artificially by Dr. James Naismith as an acceptable "noncontact" indoor sport in 1892, and since excessive roughness is penalized by the rules, it has often been accused of being a feminine game. "The game is for sissys," other critics say, and they too move on.

With the advent in the fifties of improved athletes as well as vast improvement in shooting, scores have generally risen, which prompts still other anti-basketball people to say, "Aw, they never play defense, the scores are too high."

There is, of course, absolutely nothing objective about a sports fan's likes and dislikes. You can no more convince a fan devoted to one sport of the merits of a sport that does not move him than you can impress upon an insensitive person the beauty of a sunset. A person cannot manufacture enthusiasm for a sport if in his heart he doesn't "dig it."

The cold fact is that most people in America dig basketball. They have embraced it too outside its home country; as a team sport basketball is second only in worldwide popularity to the game we refer to as "soccer."

Proponents argue that it is the artistry involved in playing the game that attracts people. Whatever the appeal, it seems to have been instantaneous: teams were paying their men to play basketball within three years after the game was invented. Promoters were no more anxious to back a fan-less operation in 1895 than they are now.

When it is well played, basketball is a precision team sport in which five men blend their talents in both offense and defense to achieve a common goal. It is also a game in which the matching of the players is almost as important as any single player's skills. The most casual YMCA three-on-three player knows how much more he enjoys the game when teamed with those he considers "smart" players. It is no different at any level—amateur, professional, or Russian.

At the same time, the truly gifted individual performer can ask for no greater showcase among team games than that provided by basketball. It has ever been thus, from the old-time stars of the teens and twenties; through the electrifying impact on the game of Stanford's Hank Luisetti; through the dominating inside play of the professional game's first great center, George Mikan; and right on up to modern artists such as Wilt Chamberlain, Connie Hawkins, Earl Monroe, and today's "ultimate showman," Julius ("Doctor J.") Erving. The important distinction remains, however: stars excite crowds, but teams win games. It is basketball's ability both to fulfill the team concept and to provide, through individual genius, the scream-your-lungs-out kind of excitement needed that has enabled it to attain its present status.

The dominant brand of basketball in its first 80 years has been that which is played in high school. Midwest states such as Indiana, Illinois, Ohio, and Iowa have school tournament traditions dating back 50 years or more. Backboards nailed to garage doors, poles, and trees are as much a symbol of midwestern America as church suppers. Naturally, it followed that those high school stars were responsible for making their colleges famous.

Along the eastern seaboard, particularly in New York City and Philadelphia, a parallel tradition was established. People of all nationalities took to a game that, unlike baseball and football, did not require tremendous space or extensive equipment. Rims and backboards could easily be put up in school yards, and no special footgear was needed. Everyone owned a pair of sneakers.

Variations in style of play, some of which exist to this day, were locally developed. Being descendants of hardy prairie folk, the midwestern boys (and, especially in Iowa, the girls) enjoyed physical contact. Rugged rebounding battles were staples of basketball there. Outside shooting was considered the best way to get the ball into the basket. Jump shots were practiced by the hour.

New Yorkers brought a sense of cunning to the game. The easiest shot was best (lowering the odds against missing), and so driving, or at least shooting from very close, was the preferred way to play. Easterners developed what is referred to today as "New York playground basketball," the staples being the so-called "give-and-go" and the ever-popular "back door" play. Deception and chicanery mattered. A man did not have to be beaten to death if a subtle nudge or outright shove at the right moment could spring the "nudger" free for a pass. This is not to say that New Yorkers couldn't handle the rough stuff when the occasion demanded. But why go up the river for assault and battery if you can pick the guy's pocket instead?

Easterners (Philadelphians as well as New Yorkers) and midwesterners shared one common theory about shooting: the only thing you do with one hand is scratch. All shooting was done with both hands firmly on the basketball.

The few professional teams that existed before the mid-forties were, for the most part, barnstormers. They speak of the "dance hall" days of professional basketball. And they meant it. Often, the only place two pro teams could find in which to play was a dance hall, and there they proved to be a minor attraction. Occasionally a reckless promoter or two would attempt to start a league, but it would quickly fold. One such league had as its chief attraction the original Celtics (New York, that is), who ruined the league by being much too good for it.

The basketball public was more attuned to high school and college ball, where drama was sustained and players less perfect than the pros. Clever professional ball handlers could prevent late comebacks by simply dribbling merrily all over the court, killing the clock. So pro basketball, such as it was, stumbled along as a ninth-rate spectator attraction until after World War II.

When the boom came, it was, as so often happens, reckless. The American public, which had managed to drag itself through the first 45 years of the twentieth century with no decent professional basketball leagues, was confronted now with two, the National Basketball League, which had the best players, and the Basketball Association of America, which, on the whole, had the better arenas.

Typical of the chaos that existed was the situation in Boston. This city, now so closely connected with the sport through the magic name of the Boston Celtics, hadn't even had basketball in the city's school system for a 20-year period. In the winter it was a second-generation hockey town. The Boston Celtics came into being only because there was a need to fill empty dates in Boston Garden. Local basketball interest was hardly a factor.

With the exception of a few gifted players who chose to remain ''amateur'' by playing in the National Industrial Basketball League (Phillips 66ers, Peoria Caterpillars, for example), the best players

Second only to soccer in worldwide popularity as a team sport, basketball is a game of artistry and motion.

in the world were playing in one of the two new leagues. It was the first time professional basketball had proved lucrative enough for quality collegians to consider playing full time. If pro basketball had any chance of becoming a force in the American sports picture, it had to happen then and either through the auspices of the BAA or the NBL.

There is an adage that "nothing succeeds like success." Thus, the best way for pro basketball to establish itself would be by promoting a successful product. Which they did. Much of what basketball is today and will be tomorrow is to the credit of George Mikan and the Minneapolis Lakers, the first great "modern" professional basketball team.

The Lakers began in the NBL, where they met with immediate success. But by 1948, the league was crumbling, losing both talented players and franchises to the BAA, which had greater financial resources. Finally, in 1948, its prize possession, the Lakers, went over to the newly named National Basketball Association. They captured the championship in the 1948–49 season and won it in four of the next five seasons.

Whatever meager exposure the NBA received outside of New York City in those days was due to the Lakers, and especially the spectacled Mikan, then the finest center in basketball. Though the Laker era only spanned six calendar years, the team experienced a complete personnel turnover between the first championship year of 1948–49 and the last, 1953–54. The only exception was Mikan. (Incidentally, the only common playing link between the 1956–57 champion Celtics and the 1968–69 champion Celtics was

Bill Russell, who succeeded Mikan as pro basketball's dominating force.)

Had there not been a magic team and a magic player like number "99" (the number alone made Mikan unique) and had there been a series of undistinguished title clubs, it is possible that the public, which had not exactly clamored for professional basketball, would have ignored the enterprise. But people were curious about these Yankee-like Minneapolis Lakers. And the rest of the league rolled along behind them.

Mikan was tall (6-10) and relatively immobile by today's standards. He used his weight to great advantage, and he was virtually unstoppable inside when he wheeled in for a hook shot. Given today's wider foul lane (when he began playing, it was 6 feet wide; it is now 16 and could be increased), he could not be as effective in the NBA as we know it today.

There were other big, heavy men in his day, just as there are 7-footers other than Kareem Abdul-Jabbar today. However, none of them approached Mikan's level of play—perhaps because they lacked his competitive zeal. Mikan combined ability with brains and, most importantly, desire. Alongside him in the peak Minneapolis years was the forerunner of today's balanced front court, the excellent forward pair of rugged Vern Mikklesen and clever Jim Pollard. For guards the Lakers had the great Slater Martin, one of the best playmakers and defensive players of all time, and the capable Whitey Skoog. When they played well, which was most of the time, no team in basketball could touch them.

The Lakers remained on top as long as Mikan was Mikan. When he began to slip, they fell

Shooters and strongmen like Luisetti
and Mikan (especially Mikan) kept
the early pro leagues going, but today's
game is based on speed and ingenuity,
learned sometimes on baked dirt
back yards, sometimes in the inner city.

Today there are electronic scoreboards,
two flourishing leagues, and high
salaries. It wasn't always that way.

too. By 1955 they were finished as a great team.

Despite their string of championships and the steady stream of great collegiate players filtering into the NBA, the league was not able to attain full respectability. Indeed, had it not been for the ingenious institution of the 24-second rule prior to the 1953–54 season, the league might have perished. There continued to be a dearth of quality black players in the league. Many teams were reluctant to use blacks for fear of offending their paying customers. In addition, the Harlem Globetrotters, then at the peak of their competitive level, were able to outbid NBA teams for outstanding black talent. Into this fuzzy atmosphere arrived Bill Russell, tall and black, who would turn the Boston Celtics into the most famous basketball team in history.

The record books reveal that the Celtics won 11 league championships in the next 13 years, but what the Celtics really were as a team far transcended the figures. The Celtics personified all that was exciting in basketball. They were the first team to combine aggressive team defense and fast break basketball. With Arnold "Red" Auerbach at the helm, the Celtics were able to demonstrate the value of team basketball while maintaining in their stars the individual traits that made them such distinct talents. Auerbach had a combative personality. It was said of him, "You can take the boy out of Brooklyn, but you can't take Brooklyn out of the boy." Red was a bad loser. As a winner, he was unbearable.

With national television coverage increasing all the time, the Celtics quickly became the nation's team: Russell grabbing a rebound or blocking a shot; Bob Cousy starting a fast break with a behind-the-back pass; Tom Heinsohn firing an eerie line drive jumper or hooking from the corner; Bill Sharman coming off a pick for a soft jumper; Frank Ramsey entering the game and scoring two quick baskets before the opponents realize he's

there; the Jones boys, Sam and K. C., pressing rivals all over the court, scoring easy baskets after numerous steals; Jim Loscutoff setting a bruising pick or scattering bodies on a rebound; Auerbach himself stomping his foot after an official's adverse call, waving his rolled-up scorecard, arguing jowl to jowl with Sid Borgia or lighting his patented "victory" cigar. These sights became ingrained in the consciousness of America's basketball fans.

Always there was the fast break. Auerbach had been an advocate of up-tempo basketball from his first coaching days, but he had been stymied in his first five years in Boston because he lacked the strong rebounder necessary to trigger his potentially great running game. One basketball saying goes, "You can't run without the ball," and nobody was more acutely aware of that fact than the fiery Auerbach.

With Russell, an All-American at the University of San Francisco and an Olympic hero, Auerbach got his fast break. Red was lucky to get him. He didn't have the draft rights, but he obtained them from the St. Louis Hawks in a trade for his incumbent center, ("Easy") Ed McCauley, and a man who would go on to become one of the game's great small forwards, Cliff Hagan. All the deal gave him, however, was the right to negotiate with Russell. He had to beat out the then powerful Harlem Globetrotters and their shrewd owner, Abe Saperstein, in order to sign him.

Signing Russell did not prove to be difficult. Any man who had led his college team to successive NCAA titles and then given his country an Olympic basketball title possessed enough pride to want to play in the world's strongest basketball league rather than become a full-time clown.

The rest, as they say, is history. Only twice in Russell's 13-year NBA career did he not play on a championship team. The first time was in 1957–58, his second year. He sprained an ankle in the final series against St. Louis and without him the

Celtics succumbed in six games. Still, the Hawks needed a playoff-record 50 points by Bob Pettit in the final game to eliminate the Russell-less Celtics. The second time was in 1967, when the awesome Philadelphia 76ers, led by Wilt Chamberlain, simply overpowered and outplayed everyone they met, the Celtics included.

The Celtics grew and matured together, and in their playing raised the artistic level of the game. Like the Yankees and Canadiens, the only other professional athletic teams ever in their class, they were flexible. Just as the Yankees were always sound defensively and had strong pitching in addition to their solid hitting, just as the Canadiens always had a first-rate goalkeeper and smart defensemen to augment their explosive scorers, so did the Celtics have exceptional balance. The watchword was always "team." Seldom did a Celtic name appear among the top 10 scorers, but seldom did the Celtics fail to score the most points as a team. Their offense was as capable when setting up as it was when the team was running.

As a visible symbol of excellence, the Celtics spawned their requisite share of imitators. Every little man soon became a mini-Cousy, much to the despair of countless high school and college coaches, who much preferred that their guards pass the ball in a conventional manner to increase

As a visible symbol of excellence, the
Celtics spawned their requisite share of
imitators. Every little man became a
mini-Cousy—to the despair of coaches.

19

its chances of arriving on target. Young forwards began tossing hooks from all angles in emulation of Heinsohn. Throughout America, young men, both black and white, looked up to Russell, a man worthy of respect off the court as well as on.

Subsequent events have revealed that such talent as they possessed cannot be manufactured. In the first 11 years after Cousy's 1963 retirement, for example, only one legitimate heir to Cousy's flamboyant, yet essentially wise, floor play has surfaced, and that man is Ernie DiGregorio. Heinsohn's swashbuckling corner play has simply not been equaled, and there have been very few sincere imitators. As for Russell, who can express surprise that no plethora of youngsters possessing his reflexes, brains, and winning spirit has descended upon us? What the Celtics were and how far ahead of their contemporaries (and perhaps their successors) they were may never be effectively calculated.

From 1959 on the Celtics' dominance was constantly threatened by teams led by Chamberlain, who may very well have been the most imposing physical being ever to step onto a basketball court—or into any athletic arena, for that matter. Almost immediately, Chamberlain and Russell were seen as individuals, detached from the other four men on their teams. As much as their coaches and the two men themselves protested that their duels were merely a part of the whole spectacle, the press and public were not convinced. When Boston won, Russell had won. When Philadelphia (or, later, San Francisco or Los Angeles) won, Chamberlain was the better man.

Given that Russell's so-called "supporting cast" was better, it came as no surprise to discerning viewers that Boston won a lot more games than did Chamberlain's teams. Wilt could not truthfully claim he had no help, but it wasn't until the 1966–67 season that he brought it all together and played with a truly dominating team.

Signing Russell did not prove to be difficult. Only twice in his 13-year career did he not play on a championship team.

20

The team was the Philadelphia 76ers. The franchise had moved from Syracuse in 1963 after 14 years in New York, where it had been a perennial contender and one-time (1955) champion. Chamberlain had been traded from the San Francisco Warriors to Philadelphia in 1965 for guard Paul Neumann, center Connie Dierking, the rights to retired forward Lee Shaffer, and cash. Immediate evidence of his impact on the franchise was the fact that the 76ers, a 40–40 team in the 1964–65 regular season, carried the Celtics to seven games in the eastern playoff finals, and were finally denied victory in a one-point game when John Havlicek alertly stole an in-bounds pass from Hal Greer to Chet Walker with three seconds left.

The team played well enough to defeat the Celtics by one game in the regular season the following year, but the more experienced Celtics unit blasted the 76ers out in five games when the playoff confrontation came. By the next year, Philadelphia was ready.

The starting five consisted of Walker (then, as now, a premier one-on-one player) at forward, along with hulking Lucious Jackson, a monstrous man whose potentially brilliant career was cut short by a crippling Achilles tendon tear. The guards were crafty Hal Greer and electrifying (if you liked him) or obnoxious (if you hated him) Wally Jones. Chamberlain, who averaged 45 minutes of playing time a game, was the only center they would ever need. The all-important sixth man was a 23-year-old leaping fool named Billy Cunningham. Other prime subs were veteran forward Dave Gambee, youthful guards Matt Guokas and Bill Melchionni, and aging (and frequently injured) guard Larry Costello. The coach was Alex Hannum, who, in 1958, with the St. Louis Hawks, was the last man to beat the Celtics in the playoffs.

Though Celtics fans considered the very

A strong case can be made for the 1966-67 76ers being the greatest team for one season in the league's history.

thought anathema, a strong case can be made for the 1966–67 76ers being the greatest team for one season in the history of the league. Along with the 1972–73 Celtics, they were certainly the most consistent. Compiling a 69–13 regular season record, they never won more than 11 games in a row. Their longest losing streak was 3; they also had one of 2. On the morning of January 30, 1967, they had a 47–4 record (in a 10-team league before anyone had ever heard of the ABA).

Philadelphia had every available weapon. Scoring could come from anywhere. The per-game averages of the Big Six ranged from Jackson's 12.0 to Chamberlain's 24.1. Wilt led the league in rebounds and Walker, Cunningham, and Jackson each averaged over seven rebounds a game. The 76ers were first in the league in offense, third in defense.

Chamberlain was the key. The big man was at his peak then and was well into the second phase of his multi-tiered career. Phase one was his offensive stage. He shot virtually every time he received the ball and set scoring standards that, most likely, will never be matched, especially his 50.4 per-game average in 1961–62. Sometime after the team's move to San Francisco he entered into what can be termed his all-around phase. By 1967 he had it down, and in that glorious season he was the greatest one-season center ever. He scored 24.1 points per game, surpassed that figure with 24.2 rebounds, and was third in the league with 7.8 assists. Defensively, he was mobile and thoroughly imposing, his 7-foot 1-inch frame swatting away countless shots and his very presence scaring away countless others. By the following season, however, the inscrutable Chamberlain had entered into phase three, his non-shooting period. This stage culminated in the 1972–73 season, when he made 72.7 percent of all his field goal attempts, almost 95 percent of which were no longer than three feet.

The only blemish on Philadelphia's otherwise uncluttered victory canvas was a 4–5 regular season record against the Celtics, who, in Russell, had the one man who could adequately cope with Chamberlain in most situations.

Vindication for Chamberlain, his 76er teammates, and hundreds of thousands of long-suffering Philadelphians came on the night of April 11, 1967, when the 76ers eliminated the Celtics with a 140–116 rout to take the Eastern Division finals in five games. All that is beautiful and, at the same time, frightening about the power and spectacle of professional basketball was on display that evening.

The over ten thousand people who crowded creaky old Convention Hall in Philadelphia had not come just to see a basketball game; they had come to see a trial, execution, and burial. The Celtics to them were far more than opponents. They were, quite literally, "The Enemy," an enemy guilty of 10 years worth of war crimes, for whom a bloody death was much too civilized. And at some point that night the crowd subtly became a mob.

They were enraged when Boston took a 16-point first half lead, but when Wally Jones opened up the third period with four consecutive twisting downtown jumpers (he was once described as a man whose shot "looks like someone struggling to get out of a manhole"), they were as fired up as a hound dog who has just picked up the scent. It was Jones who incited the crowd. "Take that, you bastards!" each of those jumpers seemed to say. And when he came back from a solitary miss to make four more of those howitzers in the deciding third period, the crowd was fully unleashed. No matter what the 76ers gave, they wanted more.

Though a final coup was hardly needed, one was nonetheless provided. Boston's Bailey Howell went up for a jumper at the top of the key, and Jackson, all 6 feet 9 inches and 240 pounds of him, simply smashed the ball back to earth as though it were a child's balloon. Big Luke then dribbled downcourt and nearly tore down the backboard with a vengeful two-hand stuff. The noise that broke from the crowd seemed enough to wake slumbering New Jersey suburbanites across the Delaware River.

With the destruction of the Celtics, the 76ers felt their job was done. The mere fact that they had ended Boston's championship string at eight straight was enough to insure them a place in basketball history. They were less than overpowering in the ensuing final series against San Francisco, but even half an effort was good enough for them to win the title in six games.

After a bitter disappointment in the 1968 playoffs, when the 76ers allowed Boston to come back from a 3–1 deficit to win the Eastern Division championship, Chamberlain was traded to Los Angeles, where he was to play on another champion, the truly great Los Angeles Lakers of 1971–72. The 76ers began a steady decline that ended in the embarrassment of a 9–73 season in 1972–73.

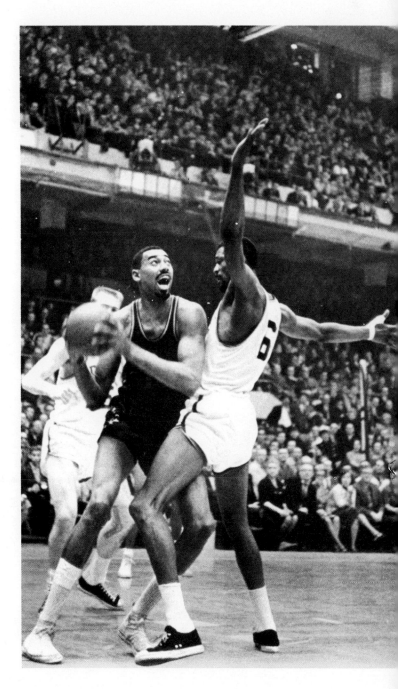

Chamberlain was the key. The big man was at his peak then and was well into the second phase of his career.

In between the 68–13 76ers of 1966–67 and the 69–13 Lakers of 1971–72 was the first championship of another legitimately great team, the New York Knicks. Playing in New York, the communications center of the world and the most important city in any professional sports league, the Knicks had greater influence on the growth of the league than any other team, the Celtics included. When, with an early season streak of 18, the 1969–70 Knicks broke the then league record of 17 consecutive games won, the publicity dam broke. The Knicks, and therefore the league, were a hot item.

The Knicks were somewhat similar to the old Celtics in both the way they moved the ball on offense and the way they played exemplary team defense. There was one crucial distinction, however. Whereas Boston was the greatest fast-breaking team in history, the Knicks didn't run much.

The Knicks, like the Celtics, also had vivid personalities. Dave DeBusschere was the workingman's player, a solid citizen who simply went out and banged away in order to accomplish his task. Though he wasn't the best or most consistent shooting forward in the league, or the most effective rebounder or passer, he was more than adequate in all departments. In one area, the demanding art of playing defense, he was the best.

His corner partner, Bill Bradley, was a legend at age 21. An All-American from Princeton and a Rhodes Scholar, Bradley was a miserable failure as a guard, where his slender 6-foot 5-inch frame first dictated he should play. It was discovered, however, that most forwards despaired of running with or after him, and that, when combined with DeBusschere, an equally cerebral player, he was an excellent "small" forward.

At center the Knicks called on sturdy Willis Reed, a 6-foot 9-inch, 240-pound competitor who was accomplished enough to have played in All-Star games as a forward when his true position was center. Along with Dave Cowens, he may very

Playing in New York, the communications center of the world, the Knicks had greater influence on the growth of the league than any other team.

well have been the most versatile of centers. He could shoot from the outside, had excellent inside moves, could put the ball on the floor and drive exceptionally well to the basket, was a ferocious rebounder, played aggressive defense, put out far more than the average effort at all times, and was most dangerous in any of these categories in clutch situations. In 1969–70, his contemporaries voted him the Most Valuable Player.

One starting guard was sleepy-eyed Dick Barnett, who talked jive and gave the distinct impression that the only book he had ever read was the Knicks' press guide, but who, in fact, was an intellectual. He played chess by mail and eventually acquired a master's degree. He was a superb middle distance shooter, a great driver, and a dogged defensive player, the perfect straight man for the "star of the show," Walt Frazier.

Frazier was the bandleader, the orchestrator. "It's Clyde's ball," explained Reed. "He just lets the rest of us play with it sometimes." Nicknamed "Clyde" because of his elaborate "Bonnie-and-Clyde"-style wardrobe, Frazier was establishing himself as the best all-around guard in basketball. Ironically, his greatest fame came for an alleged defensive prowess he did not possess. Though famed for his alertness and ability to make steals ("I can catch flies with my bare hands," he boasted), he was only a so-so straight-up defender. His effectiveness was in the way he blended with the other four on defense. Watching the way Barnett covered for him, and he for Barnett, and Reed for both of them, was an exhilarating experience for New York basketball aficionados. Strangely, Frazier's amazing offense ability was often dismissed, even when the eventual absence of Reed and Barnett revealed his proficiency.

Each man's game was marked by a similar characteristic that far transcended his individual specialty. Again rivaling the Celtics (the ultimate compliment), the team's greatest asset was the

There seemed to be no situation too involved for the Knicks to cope with. It was this intellectual aspect of their play that endeared them to the fans.

ability of each player to think on the court. Basketball is a game of shifting moods, momentums, and trends. It is also a game requiring instant judgments. And there seemed to be no situation too involved for the Knicks to cope with. It was this intellectual aspect of their play that endeared them so to the intense Madison Square Garden fans. They knew that, while leapers were available by the truckloads, complete players usually come one to a crate. They had five—a dream come true.

For a five-year period from the 1969–70 season through the 1973–74 campaign, the Knicks were the best team in professional basketball. They averaged 53 victories a year, won two championships, lost a third in the finals when DeBusschere got hurt, and were severely crippled by another injury to DeBusschere on another occasion. They were basketball's foremost "money" team, and they were generally held up as the standard of team excellence at both ends of the floor. Had Reed's career not come to a premature end in 1974, they might very well have continued.

**The Knicks, led by guard Walt Frazier,
were finally challenged by Los
Angeles, and their guard, Jerry West.**

During the "Knicks Era," with almost no warning or advance publicity, the Lakers of 1971–72 annihilated the competition, winning 69 games and the playoff championship.

Coached by Bill Sharman, who had previously won championships in both the ill-fated American Basketball League and the rival American Basketball Association, and powered by Chamberlain, who became Southern California's reigning cult figure because of his yellow headband, the Lakers accomplished what many people feel was the single greatest team feat in the history of American professional sports. From November 5, 1972, through January 7, 1973, they won 33 consecutive games.

The Lakers fit the classic mold of a great team in that they were well-balanced offensively, had a great center, and were defensively oriented. The 35-year-old Chamberlain concentrated on rebounding and defending, pouring virtually all his energy into it. With three excellent shooters in Jerry West, Gail Goodrich, and forward Jim McMillian, and with a rugged offensive rebounder and dangerous inside threat in "Happy" Hairston, Chamberlain was only rarely called on to be a primary offensive weapon. He limited himself to tap-ins and occasional backhand flips (what Los Angeles announcer Chick Hearn called "finger rolls"), completely abandoning the fadeaway jumper he employed often in his younger days.

Sharman was also able to get something out of Wilt that none of his previous coaches could. Somehow he sold Chamberlain on the virtues of the quick outlet pass to start the Los Angeles fast break. Wilt took great pride in throwing long touchdown passes to Goodrich and Hairston, two of the most accomplished "cheaters" (that is, men who take off for the other end as soon as a rival launches a shot) in NBA history. The added threat enhanced Los Angeles' effectiveness by at least 20 percent.

The Lakers were more like the strong 76er team than like either the Knicks or the Celtics. It wasn't simply the presence of Chamberlain as the center on both teams; rather, it was the absence of a team personality. Neither the 76ers nor the Lakers ever made visual poetry out of basketball as the Celtics and Knicks did. The inescapable conclusion is that both the Celtics and Knicks, at their best, would always be able to handle a Chamberlain-led team. As for the outcome of a vintage Celtics–Knicks confrontation, the only possible edge would be Boston's bench.

It is a paradox in basketball that what is the dullest may also be the most efficient; what is the most eye-catching may be the least productive. When a team manages to combine an appeal to the emotional, artistic, and critical side of the discerning viewer, it becomes something special. Therefore, no discussion of great teams in basketball is complete without mention of a team that never won a championship, the Baltimore Bullets.

Circumstance and luck play inordinately large roles in determining modern day championship outcomes, and so it was that the Bullets were never favored by the gods with a title. Rarely, however, has a legitimately outstanding team provided the vast number of thrills-per-minute that this gifted Bullet team did. In the sheer matter of style, they may have set unreachable standards.

Conceived as an expansion team in Chicago in 1961, the Bullets moved to Baltimore after two fruitless campaigns and took up residence in last place in the Eastern Division. They were always making trades—but with the same end results. Victories proved hard to come by.

They began assembling the proper pieces in 1963, when they induced Gus Johnson to forsake his last year of collegiate eligibility at the University of Idaho and join the team. The powerfully built 6-foot 6-inch forward became an outstanding player and, more interestingly, a dynamic one.

Rarely has any outstanding team provided the vast number of thrills-per-minute that the gifted Bullets team did. In the matter of style, they may have set unreachable standards.

With his huge hands he proved a fascinating ball handler. He'd pluck rebounds one-handed, wave the ball around as though it were a grapefruit, and throw superb behind-the-back passes for longer distances than anyone else in the league.

He was a good medium-range shooter, but what he did best was drive to the basket. He invented a move known as the "Step and Stuff," in which he took off farther from the basket than anyone believed humanly possible and smashed the ball through the hoop. He loved to show off, and the crowd loved to see him do it. He was not all flash, however. He was a dominating cornerman rebounder, twice grabbing over a thousand rebounds, an impressive total for a forward. He was twice named to the NBA's All-Defensive first team.

On this memorable team, however, he wasn't even the leading attraction. That distinction was captured by an amazing basketball player named Earl ("the Pearl") Monroe. The basketball world first heard of Earl Monroe when he was setting all kinds of scoring records at Winston-Salem College. Scoring nights of 50 and up were commonplace for him. It wasn't too long before the scouts and media descended on the all-black school.

He joined the Bullets in 1967, but he wasn't good enough to pull them out of last place. What he did do was create excitement. He did things no one had ever done in a professional basketball game, inventing moves with his near-miraculous body control.

Monroe was the master of the spin. It seemed he spent half the game spinning. He could spin at midcourt and hit a teammate with a spectacular pass right under the basket. He would back an opponent in and come off a spin for a soft jumper. There was perhaps no more helpless feeling for an NBA player than to be caught on a two-on-one or three-on-one fast break when Monroe had control of the ball.

The late sportswriting genius Jimmy Cannon

Unseld was a superb rebounder and, more importantly, he knew what to do with the ball.

It is not especially surprising, therefore, that the game has captured the imagination of artistically inclined people. Such a devotee of professional basketball is Russell Sherman, a magnificent concert pianist and faculty member of the New England Conservatory of Music in Boston. To him, basketball is a game to be savored. And he finds that his age and professional respectability have done little to diminish his emotional approach to competitive sports. "My father," he explains, "used to say, 'You cry, and they get paid. I don't understand it.' I still feel very sad when my favorite team loses." As Sherman sees it, the central issue for a fan is style versus efficiency. Stylists can be efficient, he feels, though not many of them are as good as people think. Efficient players may have a certain sense of style, but all too often it is not fully appreciated. In rare cases, a man is able to combine both qualities.

Oscar Robertson is one of the most acclaimed players of all time. "If I were going to seek a model for a young player," says Frank Power, a long-time coach of freshman basketball at Boston College and coauthor with Bob Cousy of a highly praised textbook on basketball, "I would tell him to dribble like Oscar, shoot like Oscar, and pass like Oscar. Technically, he was flawless." That opinion is shared by many people in professional basketball. Oscar was, without question, the consummate stylist.

Russell Sherman on Robinson: "I was never turned on very much by Oscar. Oscar was a great stylist, and, from an artistic point of view, extremely graceful and beautiful to watch. But he dribbled too much. I felt that in the proportions of the twenty-four-second clock the guard shouldn't be holding the ball for fourteen to eighteen seconds and then make the play at the last moment. I felt there was not enough general fluency in the motion of his talents."

**Basketball has been likened to ballet.
There are soaring leaps and
pirouettes and exquisite artistry.**

Walt Frazier's style of play has always been compared to Robertson's. "A fellow like Frazier," says Sherman, "is a stylist, which again is pleasant for me to watch. But I think there is a negative connotation, too. That is, he always plays within his style.

"I think one of the positive aspects is that he really knows how to control the tempo of the game. On the other hand, when he's in a certain mood, in terms of his defensive play, he is not making those remarkable adaptations at the remarkable rate that, I think, a Jerry West used to make or that a Don Chaney makes now. You will see dry periods with Frazier during certain games. To me, that's disappointing. While Jerry Sloan is much more limited, he is always playing at the peak of his capacity."

Another amazing stylist is Lenny Wilkens, a man who should have played in top hat, white tie, and tails. He did not have much of a jump shot, but what he accomplished offensively with a smooth one-hand set and a breathtaking display of awesome drives to the basket supplied ample scoring. As a passer, he came closer to Cousy than anyone until Ernie DiGregorio came along.

After retiring to take over the coaching job at Portland in 1974, Wilkens was un-retired in order to play for the team and, hopefully, stabilize a young, talented, but inconsistent club that had just obtained Bill Walton as its center.

"Wilkens," contends one analyst, "is very much a Fred Astaire, and that is why he is not right for Portland at present. The idea of a stylist means that there are certain identifiable traits of motion and gesture that tend to repeat themselves, which, by their descriptiveness, give that stylistic attribute. That, however, at a certain point is directly opposed to the capacity of efficiency that demands, as in Havlicek, a sort of nonpersonal, dispassionate approach that simply treats each situation as though it were a new and novel thing

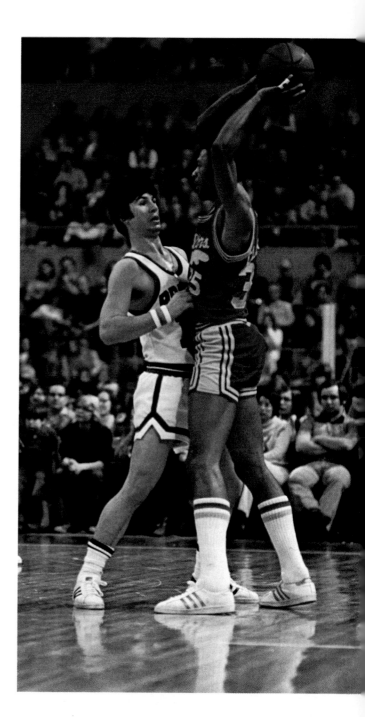

that had to be solved. That sort of person has the flexibility to be able to continuously solve each situation without registering, 'This is my way of doing it. This is my style. This is my approach.' ''

Such a repetitive person is Elvin Hayes, who, while being enormously gifted, remains unappealingly limited in his approach. ''Elvin is a stylist,'' the analyst goes on. ''He has three or four beautiful things that he does, and that's his repertoire. He goes through them and he exhausts them and then he repeats himself. It seems he's either hot or he's cold.''

Ernie DiGregorio is considered a stylist. In his first year and a quarter (before he injured his knee early in the 1974–75 season), he rarely played a succession of outstanding games, and in the infrequent times his Buffalo team played a rival, he always seemed to be held in check. Critics of pure stylists point out that you can find a pattern of defensing a stylist like DiGregorio and thus take away his efficiency.

Ernie DeGregorio is considered a stylist. He may be the best since the reign of Cousy.

45

The ultimate combination of style and efficiency may have occurred not in basketball, but in baseball, in the person of Mickey Mantle. His style depended on two things. One was that he would strike out well over a hundred times a year, which gave him a certain amount of charisma, the other that he was the only power hitter in history—maybe the only hitter in history—who could consistently beat out a bunt with two strikes, a virtuoso feat that made him a legend.

Basketball's answer to Mantle might be Dave Cowens, who could hardly help but appeal to the artistic, emotional, and dramatic side of any serious fan.

In the beginning it was hard not to see Cowens, using a rough analogy, as a Johnny McKenzie, the brawler who used to play for the Boston Bruins. Cowens, at first glance, gave the impression of a slasher, a wild man. Not as apparent is the type of person Cowens really is. Gradually, the quality of his personality revealed itself in his basketball play: his leaping, his diving for the loose ball, the incredible exhibitions of taking one-in-ten chances of making the play. He really *wanted* to make the play. He was not just living out a lifestyle of self-destructiveness.

Marv Albert, the excellent New York play-by-play announcer, has said, "I don't understand him. What is this guy doing? He does crazy things in exhibition games. He'll kill himself."

Cowens is still alive, but during the first exhibition game of the 1974–75 season, he chased Denver guard Fatty Taylor downcourt after the latter had made a steal. Though Taylor was at least 15 feet ahead of Cowens when the chase began, Cowens tried anyway. He arrived at the basket in time to block Taylor's shot, but then he kept on going—into the superstructure of the basket, jamming his foot and setting in motion a chain of events that would culminate 10 days later with his breaking a bone in the same foot. Finally, the reck-

less hero paid the price of his own personality and drive.

The contrast between Cowens, a study in unbounded kinetic energy, and Abdul-Jabbar, a stylist who believes in economy of motion and a limited output of energy, was dramatically illustrated in the 1974 playoff finals between the Celtics and the Bucks.

It was in this series that the adaptability of Cowens and, indeed, the entire Boston team prevailed over the Bucks who, symbolized by Abdul-Jabbar (whose greatest asset, his size, also proved to be his greatest liability, limiting his mobility and speed), were powerless to adjust when Boston threw new defensive challenges at them.

**Basketball's answer to Mantle
might be Dave Cowens, who could hardly help but
appeal to the emotional side of any fan.**

46

Kareem's game is an inside game. The farther away he is from the basket, the less effective he is. Likewise, he is only useful to the Bucks when he has the ball, when the entire scenario revolves around him. He is almost as good a passer as he is a shooter, and when he has the ball the Bucks increase their chances of scoring immeasurably.

Though approximately 7 feet 3 inches tall, Abdul-Jabbar is not a good rebounder. Because of his size, he has done adequately in the statistics, but he could do more. Defensively, he plays hard in spurts. There are days when he roams the court like an aggrieved Goliath searching for missing offspring behind every rival pick. Then there are days when he resembles a lifelike statue placed under the basket. Yet, because there are so few Cowenses around, Kareem generally succeeds in bringing his team a victory.

Kareem is, in short, the exact antithesis of Cowens. Yet by 1975 (he has been in the league a year longer than Cowens), each man has played center on the same number of championship teams—one. In other words, Cowens had been accomplishing something too.

Cowens is the most versatile center who has ever played the game. Against men his own size or, at least, comparable size, he plays inside and performs in a classic back-to-the-basket pivot manner. Against giants such as Abdul-Jabbar and, until he retired, Chamberlain, Cowens roams the perimeter, teasing the big fellows with soft jump shots, driving around them when they choose to come out to play him. He is a threat to score on the fast break, pounding the offensive boards and playing clever pick-and-roll or give-and-go with his teammates.

His value far transcends offense, however. He is an exceptional rebounder, possessing strength, great jumping ability, technical knowledge of positioning, extreme lateral quickness, and desire. He wants every rebound he can get, whereas Abdul-Jabbar seems to take only what comes his way, saving most of his energy for offense.

It is argued that Abdul-Jabbar thinks subconsciously that it's unbecoming for a person to throw out his elbows, to throw himself around in order to get rebounds, that it is not human or humane. It was the Rangers' hockey player Brad Park who said after his team had lost in the 1974 Stanley Cup series to Philadelphia, "If to win means to maim, then I don't want to win." That attitude may be what is affecting Abdul-Jabbar.

The 1974 Milwaukee–Boston final series came down to the seventh game. It had been a fascinating series, dominated by Boston defense, the slightly superhuman play of Havlicek, the offensive artistry of Abdul-Jabbar, and mad scientist-type coaching approaches that made it resemble Fischer versus Spassky as much as it did Celtics versus Bucks.

Boston had dominated the series, winning three games with comparative ease, losing one in overtime and one in double overtime, the last on a stunning Abdul-Jabbar 17-foot hook from the right corner with three seconds left, after it appeared that a magnificent overtime performance by Havlicek had wrapped up the title for Boston.

The final game was to be in Milwaukee. The Bucks were favored, perhaps only because a Celtic victory would have given them three consecutive playoff victories on the road, an unprecedented achievement.

The basis of the game turned out to be this: The Celtics elected to do something they had steadfastly avoided doing for four years. They sagged continually on Abdul-Jabbar, surrounding him with as many men as they could. In doing so, they knew their only worry was the reaction of the other four men.

Because he is 7 feet 3 inches tall, and be-

cause his entire offensive is an inside game, Kareem was incapable of making an adjustment. He could only set up close to the basket and hope his mates could give him the ball. Cowens, meanwhile, was running all over the court to pop in long jumpers. Kareem went scoreless in a crucial 17-minute span of the second and third periods, while Cowens was hitting on 8 of 13 shots. Boston won, 102–87.

The Celtics had beaten Abdul-Jabbar at every turn. They took away his offense. With their mobile center firing away at long range, they also took away his defense. As usual, they didn't worry about his rebounding. And his passing was no problem because his teammates couldn't give him the ball.

It was a tribute to the game of basketball that the heralded irresistible force was shut down by a resourceful team. Prior opponents had been powerless to stop him. The Celtics did. The stylist had been beaten.

Abdul-Jabbar is a stylist who believes in economy of motion and a limited output of energy. Kareem's game is an inside game.

Will a healthy Bill Walton be better than Abdul-Jabbar when all the returns are in?

Some argue that Walton's potential is greater. Walton, they say, has the quality of adaptation, a mark of athletic superiority. Walton can adjust and will adjust to the fact that his basic *raison d'etre* is that one is a pacifist, one eats vegetables, one has to hand the ball off, one is not supposed to take too many shots, and so forth. All this is going to hurt his team in the beginning, until he becomes more egotistical about shooting the ball or going to the offensive boards. Eventually his moves will be more comprehensive and he will be able to adjust to any situation, an ability Abdul-Jabbar does not have. Kareem does magnificent things, but repeats them. Thus goes the argument.

Hopefully it will soon be evident that the consummate battle of the seventies will be Walton versus Cowens. Each is a highly versatile and unselfish center whose primary value to his team lies in the number of ways he can help bring about victory. Each is a known competitor. While Walton does not dive over press tables nor spend a great deal of time on the floor, he is a master rebounder and an exponent of without-the-ball movement on offense.

"The excitement of the confrontation," Sherman suggests, "as it is in any basketball match-up, is compounded by the fact that it has to take place within the confines of twenty-four seconds. The way the game is constituted now, their relationship will have to be refined over a period of two to three years before they really know each other. Until they learn patterns of response to one another, the first impressions are apt to be ragged. One night Walton clearly seems superior and the next Cowens has it all over him."

Some followers of the pro game see a disturbing change in the overall atmosphere, despite the fact that the physical talents of players today are far superior to those of yesterday's players. They analyze the situation in almost a sociological context. They point to the movies that are currently popular—ships upside down, plane crashes, earthquakes, holocausts. Must we contemplate something parallel to that need for excitement in basketball? Isn't it possible that in these times inflation in general, salaries, agents, playoffs, and the speed and pressure of the game itself are creating a chaos and flux that makes it almost impossible for basketball to stress the virtues and skills of its game as an art?

Foremost among a true fan's aesthetic loves are those players who have, quite literally, broken aspects of the game down into a science, and who consider mental preparation as important as certain physical gifts. Under this heading would be such masters as Jerry West, John Havlicek, David DeBusschere, Chet Walker, Jerry Sloan, and Don Nelson. A primary link among them is concentration. Jerry West was impressive in this regard, having both intensity and control. He could always adapt.

DeBusschere, who was as far from a stylist as ever played in the league (at least among the stars), occupies a special place in Russell Sherman's heart. "To me, he did not have an athletic body. He couldn't run very well or jump. He had a very good eye but, even then, there were better shooters. But he made the most of everything he had, as does Nelson, and, somewhat similarly, Chet Walker.

"Bob Pettit also personified that quality of unselfish dedication, intensity, or energy that goes beyond the sport itself. Controlled power is what I find beautiful, and Pettit did exactly what he had to do to help his team. He didn't try dribbling the ball on his head, for example, since that had nothing to do with winning a game. He played his role beautifully."

50

Some argue that Walton's potential is greater. He is able to adapt, which is a mark of athletic superiority.

Many people feel that the present-day master of any situation is Havlicek, who emerged from the shadow of Jerry Lucas at Ohio State to become the finest all-around player in the history of the game. Although he is best remembered for his tangible contributions—any man who scores over twenty thousand points in a career cannot exactly go unnoticed, unless his name is Walt Bellamy—what makes Havlicek unique is his mental approach to the game, which can best be described by relating this incident:

The Celtics were playing a home playoff game against Atlanta, and Havlicek was ahead of the field when Atlanta's speedy Harm Gilliam caught up to him. He hit John in the air, and for a split second it seemed inevitable that Havlicek would wind up injured, perhaps seriously, as there appeared to be no way for him to avoid landing on his neck. Yet when the collision occurred, Havlicek got right up, as if nothing had happened. Later he explained that he had sensed someone was there and that his immediate response was to prepare for a fall by pulling in his arms and neck to make sure he took the fall right on his behind.

Many people feel that the present-day master of any situation is Havlicek. What makes him unique is his mental approach.

All this thinking took place while he was in the air.

It had been an inner anticipation, pre-digested 1,001 times, that took care of the situation, which was most likely to occur in a playoff. "Gilliam can't guard me and he's going to try in some unconscious way to get me out of action and I have to be ready." So, without even pondering it, Havlicek was ready.

Such a reaction is characteristic of the superior athlete. Players who can adapt are the successful ones. The rest will forever remain limited. Talent is indeed enough to insure success on lower levels; talent alone can, in fact, guarantee a certain degree of success in the professional ranks as well. But there has to be some reason why many players who can run, jump, and shoot remain on career-long treadmills.

Basketball is at its most cerebral—as well as at its most physical—level in the National Basketball Association. "That's why," one fan suggests, "I'm wondering if the fabulous Doctor J. is heading for the illustrious career that has been promised. All his individual moves spice up a game but have nothing to do with the efficiency that makes a team win or lose. If Erving plays a reasonably good game, and then puts on a few of those moves, that's all the better.

"But I think the danger with him is that his style is almost a caricature, that he is not recognized unless he is doing some extraordinary thing, and therefore he only becomes an interesting part of the game when he has the opportunity to display his *tours de force*."

This is not to say there is anything wrong with what Dr. J. does on the court, just as there was nothing wrong with anything the fabulous Bullets did on the floor. It may be, however, that excessively flashy shows of individual skill are somehow antithetical to the purpose ostensibly at hand; namely, to win ball games.

If the game is to flourish and survive, therefore, it must be on a team basis. The disappointing NBA one-on-one contests proved that. As dynamic as an individual move may be, with constant repetition it becomes meaningless. Basketball is a great game because team concepts will always prevail over individual duels. The game could never have captured the imagination of an aesthetic such as Russell Sherman, concert pianist, or the millions of truck drivers, waitresses, insurance salesmen, movie actors, clergymen, lawyers, secretaries, housewives, college professors, and executives if this weren't so.

There are problems. Excessively long schedules and drawn-out playoffs, combined with limited practice time and increasingly unsound fundamental skills of the otherwise more physically gifted athletes, have contributed to a large number of uninspired games. As a game it was better executed years ago, but it wasn't played as well. "The weakness of this game," Sherman notes, somewhat dourly, "is the possibility of this chaos, this flux, without purpose.

"The game," he continues, "when played by the best teams, does define a certain streamlined energy that is powerful. The trick is to reduce the number of possibilities for the game's breaking down. This true excellence can only, however, come from the best teams, and, unfortunately, from those teams at a time when eighty-two games have gone by—in other words, in the playoffs."

Meanwhile, Russell Sherman keeps coming back for those 82 games before the playoffs. "Great athletes," he feels, "have, among other things, the capacity to accept defeat. I watch them play and my hope is renewed that somehow, win or lose, they ultimately have a 'we're-all-in-this-thing-together' feeling. The entire exercise then becomes an exhilarating exhibition of fantasy—the true art form that is basketball."

"The game when played by the best teams becomes an exhilarating exhibition of fantasy—the true art form that is basketball."

Mayhem Begins off the Ball
Referees

2

asketball, as a visual and hopefully aesthetic experience is incomplete without the two men around whom the players seem to weave their plays—the referees.

Someone once said that "umpiring is the only profession in which a man must start out perfect and get better." The same can be said for officials in all sports, but the pressure is greater on some than it is on others—especially basketball's referees.

Football, for instance, is a picnic. Not one fan in a thousand knows what constitutes offensive holding or what an offensive team must do in order to be accused of drawing the defensive team offside. They can scream about an occasional pass interference or face mask or clipping call, but they are yelling at a distant figure with a hat on, a person whom they wouldn't recognize if they bumped into him on the street. Even the baseball umpire, whose job at home plate is probably the single toughest officiating task in organized professional sports, is anonymous to the fans.

Basketball and hockey referees, on the other hand, stand all but naked in an indoor arena, their every feature visible to every fan. Being only human, they will naturally feel far more pressure when they make their decisions, because they are far more real to the crowd than are their football and baseball counterparts. It takes true courage to disallow a Walt Frazier basket in Madison Square Garden in front of 19,694 fans and call an offensive foul on him instead.

Compared to a basketball

referee, ax murderers and tax collectors are citizen favorites. A referee's greatest satisfaction is supposed to come from not having been noticed. Some job.

Rule interpretation is but a minor part of his duties, although he certainly had better know the rules. The overwhelming portion of his calls will be judgment calls, where he must decide whether or not one player fouled another.

Life would be simple for an official if the game were played by polite gentlemen who were always trying their best not to commit a foul and who graciously acknowledged an error when it was noted. Instead, in the eyes of the two referees, basketball is played by ten thugs who are trying to do something illegal every second they are on the court, who do as much as they can get away with, and who, finally, always deny that they have done anything wrong at all.

Officiating basketball at any level is a difficult job, because it is a fast-moving game played on a relatively small surface, and because it can quickly become an emotional game. The game can be handled a bit more easily on a school basis, if only because many teams employ the zone defense, which generally allows for fewer personal fouls. In addition, younger players are less likely to commit the type of rebounding fouls that occur at higher levels.

The college game is complicated by the rules governing advancement of the ball in the front court. There being no shot clock in college, the rules makers have attempted to reduce the possibility of a stall by making it mandatory for the offensive team to advance the ball past a line painted on the court 25 feet from the basket within five seconds after

crossing midcourt, and any five seconds after bringing the ball out from in front of that line thereafter. Further, a player who is dribbling without advancing or one who is not dribbling and, in either case, is being "closely guarded" by a defender must get rid of the ball within five seconds or face a jump ball.

Counting off these infractions are a large part of a collegiate official's job. Fortunately they are one headache professional referees don't have, though most would gladly take on that problem in exchange for some of the ones they do have.

Consider the things a referee is responsible for every time the ball is brought downcourt in a professional game:

1. He must count for a five-second in-bounds violation on the part of the offensive team.

2. He must count for a ten-second backcourt violation on the part of the offensive team. Once the ball is passed in, the offensive team must advance the ball past the midcourt line within that time span.

3. He must watch to see that the ball is not passed from the front court to the backcourt once it has gone over the midcourt line. If it does, he must signal a backcourt violation.

4. He must watch for a three-second violation on the part of the offense. No offensive player can remain within the 16-foot width of the foul lane longer than three seconds.

5. He must watch for a 24-second violation on the part of the offensive team, making certain that the shot has left the player's hand prior to either the expiration of the time or the sound of the buzzer. He must also make certain that any shots taken hit the rim or the backboard, because if they don't, the 24-second countdown must continue. Sometimes clock operators make honest mistakes, and sometimes they blatantly cheat; the referee must be aware of what happens to the shot clock in either case.

6. Especially in tight ball games (not that he shouldn't do it at any time), he must watch the clock itself on occasion to make sure it is being handled properly. One night in Chicago a few years ago, the Celtics were leading the Bulls 90–88, when Matt Guokas of the Bulls heaved a long lob pass out of bounds with two seconds remaining. Boston had the ball underneath its own basket. They got the ball in, and four or five seconds elapsed before referee Manny Gomes waved his arms and declared the game over. The clock had never moved. "I had my finger on the wrong button," the clock operator explained. Had Chicago stolen the ball and tied the game up, Tom Heinsohn might have had his fingers around the clock man's throat. Referee Gomes had acted correctly in the situation.

7. He must watch for violations, such as traveling or palming, or kicking the basketball. Some of the league's top stars have pet moves that come dangerously close to being violations. There are, for instance, any number of top guards who appear to be carrying the ball whenever they

Some of the league's top stars have pet moves that come dangerously close to being violations. A referee must watch for those—and actual violations.

start their move to the basket. There are also several big men whose feet seem to be shuffling before they put the ball on the floor to start their favorite moves.

8. He must watch for out-of-bounds calls. The action is so fast, and the size of the players so formidable, that it is often exceedingly difficult to determine off which player the ball went out of bounds. It is, however, an important call to get straight as often as possible.

9. He must be alert for the defensive three-second, or zone warning. This is especially difficult. Professional teams are incorporating zone principles more and more into their defenses, and the cries of anguish from rival coaches have grown louder and louder over the years. In the old days, a zone warning consisted simply of telling Wilt Chamberlain to leave the three-second area and guard somebody, but no longer is it a matter of the big center anchoring himself while the other four men play legitimate man-to-man defense. The zones are cleverly concealed, and they are aided by the wording of the rule, which, as of 1974, reads as follows: "When the ball has passed center court, no defensive player can guard an area of the court, instead of guarding an opponent. Penalty—warning, first offense. Thereafter, technical foul."

It doesn't say that teams can't double-team the man with the ball, but it does leave a lot of grounds for interpretation. Generally speaking, NBA officials have been instructed to make sure that defensive players stay within six feet of a member of the offensive team to avoid being penalized for guarding "an area." Six feet seems more than enough space for a team of large-sized men to form a nice, compact zone defense.

For an official to spot the modern zone, he must watch the situation closely, and thus might miss another important aspect of the play.

In order to discharge his duty properly, the referee must maintain a high level of both technical and emotional expertise. Of the two, the latter is far harder to come by.

Though everyone knows that zone defenses are illegal in the NBA—and have been since its inception in 1946—they seem to be flourishing. One of the funniest incidents in recent years occurred in Madison Square Garden during the 1974 exhibition season, when the Milwaukee Bucks and Buffalo Braves played in the first game of a double-header. Milwaukee was losing by 15 points with two minutes to play, and coach Larry Costello, who is considered by many to have constructed the league's best zone defense, had his team playing a rather obvious (illegal) zone. Buffalo's Ken Charles tried to make a move, and he lost the ball.

"How the hell," exploded Costello in laughter, "can a man try to dribble his way through a (bleeping) zone?"

10. He must make sure that teams are allowed their legitimate bonus free throws. Occasionally, he must check with the official scorer to make certain a team isn't entitled to them. Nothing is more embarrassing than having a game held up while someone points out that free throws should have been shot earlier, but that an error had been made. Most scoreboards indicate the number of team fouls per period, and the official should be aware of the number.

11. Having concerned himself with all these auxiliary items, the official must also watch for on-the-ball fouls. Did the defensive man foul the offensive man? Did the offensive player commit an offensive foul while driving for that last basket? Is the rebounder from one team entitled to have his hand on the throat of the man from the other, or is that an optical illusion?

12. He must watch for off-the-ball fouls, because that is often where future trouble starts. Players running to spots should be allowed to get there—which, however, is not to say that the defensive man doesn't have the right to cut down an

Is the rebounder from one team entitled to have his hand on the throat of the man from the other, or is that an optical illusion?

angle. A man setting a pick cannot stick out his knee, hip, or elbow to strike a defensive man cutting by, nor should he move two or three feet laterally to keep in front of the man he is trying to pick off. These are essential calls to make.

13. The worst for last: goaltending. Of all the nightmares officiating has ever had, the increased jumping ability of modern players has created the most dreaded one. Trying to determine if the defensive man has blocked a shot on its downward flight, and thus has goaltended, has added more misery to the lives of officials than almost any other rule. Officials used to say that the toughest call was the blocking-charging call, but no more. Goaltending has taken its place by a wide margin.

In order to discharge his duty properly, the referee must maintain a high level of both technical and emotional expertise. Of the two, the latter is far harder to come by. It is much easier to call a game than it is to control one, and, without control the game almost always degenerates into a farce.

The first aspect of an official's technical ability is his judgment. The simple fact of the matter is that some officials have better judgment than others, which is to say that the majority of their calls more closely fit the consensus of players, coaches, team officials, writers, broadcasters, fans, and other officials. Men like Mendy Rudolph and Richie Powers do not always make calls that please everyone, but they make more calls that cannot be debated than their contemporaries, which is one reason why they wind up working the big games more than anyone else. A major factor in determining an official's technical ability to make a proper judgment is, of course, his positioning. He cannot call what he cannot properly see.

Officials work in tandems. One is called a lead official and the other a trailer. One man is stationed under the basket, the other is near mid-

Sometimes a player will foul another deliberately, in order to prevent a sure bucket. In any case, two shots.

66

court. They are diagonally opposite each other, to better cover as much of the court as possible. A referee's viewing angle is very important. If an official is not in the proper spot, he will find himself blocked from calls by extraneous bodies.

Teaching referees the proper positioning techniques is the job of NBA Supervisor of Officials, John Nucatola. He was hired several years ago and given full authority over the ever-expanding officiating staff (as the league grows, more referees are needed). He regularly summons officials into his office for sessions, during which time he shows them films of themselves to point out what they're doing right as well as wrong on the court. As a charter referee in the old BAA, a supervisor of officials in the Eastern College Athletic Conference for 12 years, and a man who has spent 40 years in the game of basketball as a player, coach, and official, Nucatola probably knows as much about the subject of officiating as anyone.

Another technical skill a referee must have is hustle. Lazy officials don't last long in the pros. There are too many fast breaks and too many quick transitions of play for a man not interested in running to keep up with. Referees run several miles a game, and they must not only be willing to keep up, they must be able to.

The important thing about a referee's willingness to hustle is that it must remain constant throughout a game. Anyone can try hard early in a game, when the issue is in doubt, or in the late stages of a close game. Nothing is more infuriating to a player or coach, however, than a referee who thinks his job has ended when both teams have their substitutes on the floor. "Don't referee the score!" Red Auerbach used to scream at officials who were letting flagrant violations go in order to get the game over with as soon as possible. Officials must remember that young players are trying to impress the coaches, perhaps in the

expectation of earning more playing time, and that during their limited stint on the court they are entitled to the same consideration given the star of the team in his 40-plus minutes.

Professional basketball has, and always has had, a number of officials who possessed excellent technical ability, but who could not be classified as good officials. "In an empty gym," explains Nucatola, "they would be excellent. Mix the crowd in and they might have a little trouble, but they would survive. But then, introduce the players and coaches—especially the coaches—and it's all over. They can't handle it."

As well as a referee might understand and interpret the rules and as many times as he might make the "correct" call, he cannot last long in professional basketball if he can't stand the heat. And if "it gets too hot," it is John Nucatola or his ABA counterpart who must remove him from "the kitchen." Permanently. "There have been so many

men," sighs Nucatola, "who have had great technical ability, but who have had trouble. If I have any skill at all, I like to think it's that I can spot this difficulty and work to salvage their careers."

What, specifically, is the difficulty? Why isn't being able to make a high percentage of acceptable calls enough to guarantee officiating success?

The answer is that officiating a professional basketball game means to control it. The two officials must be in complete charge of the game. They cannot let players, coaches, fans, or team officials dictate to them the way the game should go. (Certain general managers have been known to sit at the press table, which in itself is practically an incitement to riot.)

Suppose, for example, that a pair of officials has worked a beautiful game for two and a half periods, but that one of them makes a controversial, and possibly incorrect, call against the home team midway through the third quarter. Naturally

**As well as a referee might
understand and interpret the rules
and as many times as he might
make the "correct" call, he cannot
last long in professional basketball
if he can't stand the heat.**

the offended team objects strenuously. Perhaps the coach or one of the players comes immediately at the referee, screaming the things that emotionally charged coaches and players scream at referees every night. The cool-headed official, properly recognizing that he has just, say, taken a basket away from that team for an alleged offensive foul that might not have been an offensive foul, allows the injured parties a chance to blow off a certain amount of steam before cutting off the discussion and ordering the game to resume.

The less effective official takes the bait immediately, slaps a technical or two on the coach or player, and subsequently sets the entire team plus a hostile crowd against him for the rest of the game.

It is not beyond the province of a good official, in fact, to admit an occasional error on the court. Being a referee also means that "sometimes you can say you're sorry." Indeed, one of the frequently cited reasons for Richie Powers' overwhelming popularity with both players and coaches is the fact that he has said on several occasions while on the court, "I blew that one."

Many officials, though they don't verbalize their error, do recognize it and attempt to make up for it in what is considered to be a bad way. Their method is the much-discussed, but seldom-admitted "give-back" call, wherein a referee who realizes that he has just blown a call and handed two points to one team attempts to equalize matters by coming up with a cheap call, giving the other team an opportunity to get its two points back. Unfortunately, "two wrongs do not make a right," even in a game.

Were all officials able to lead a test-tube existence, there would seldom be problems. But, professional basketball games are played by aggressive players, coached by near-desperate men who are in need of victories to survive, and

Perhaps the coach or one of the players comes immediately at the referee, screaming the things that emotionally charged coaches and players scream.

Goaltending. Of all the nightmares officiating has ever had, the increased jumping ability of modern players has created the most dreaded one. Trying to determine if the defensive man has blocked a shot on its downward flight, and thus has goaltended, has added more misery to the lives of officials than almost any other rule.

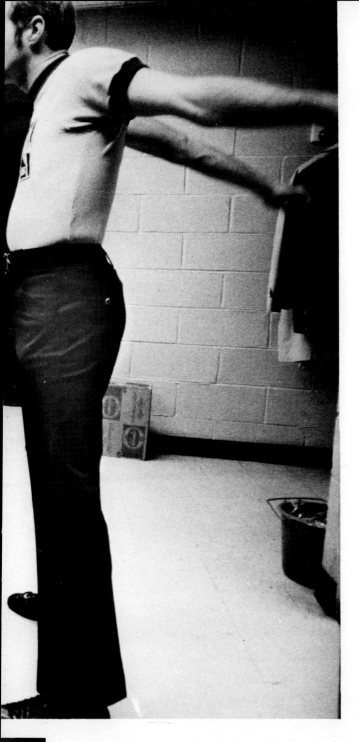

watched by maniacal fans who consider any call against their team an act of war. All the classroom training goes out the window once the game starts, and Nucatola is first to recognize that fact; he is fond of pointing out that "referees are only human."

Only an emotionally stable individual can attain and maintain success refereeing in the professional ranks. "The personality problem is the toughest," explains Nucatola. "I can teach positioning and where to go on the court, but only the man himself can learn how to act on the court."

The league devours Casper Milquetoasts. If a young official doesn't make his calls—no matter how good they are—with authority, a mental note is made and the sniping will begin. Some coaches and players will test a young official almost immediately to see if he can be manipulated. An official without presence on the court is doomed to quick extinction.

A perfect example of a young referee who burst into the league with authority is Bill Jones. He first strolled onto the floor of Madison Square Garden in October of 1973 to handle a Knicks–Celtics exhibition game with Mendy Rudolph. The usual capacity crowd was on hand to cheer for the Knicks. Working with the astute Rudolph, who often likes to take it easy during the first period when he is working with a youngster, Jones made the first four calls of the game in the first two minutes. All were against the Knicks. He also slapped a complaining Dave DeBusschere with a technical foul, which was tantamount to a young Congressman telling off the Speaker on his first day in the House of Representatives.

Perhaps the most representative example of a man who had to put his officiating game together is Jack Madden, who, after spending the beginning of his career in the NBA, is now a top ABA official. A former top athlete himself (he was the

Only an emotionally stable individual can attain and maintain success refereeing in the professional ranks. "The personality problem is the toughest."

The action is so fast, and the size of the players so formidable, that it is often exceedingly difficult to determine which player the ball went off of.

all-time leading scorer at Rider College and a pitching prospect in the Cincinnati chain until a sore arm put an end to his career), the tall (6-4), handsome Madden was a near-perfect prospect in the NBA.

He impressed observers with his knowledge and judgment but distressed them equally with his demeanor. He had what seemed to be a terminal case of "rabbit ears," and many felt that he harbored grudges against coaches with whom he'd had difficulty. One season he had constant run-ins with Butch van Breda Kolff to the point where he deserved censure as much as the fiery coach.

"I had to straighten him out," recalls Nucatola, "because he was such a good prospect. I called him in several times and told him, 'You're excellent technically, as good as anybody on my staff. But I can't afford the luxury of your irritations. Basketball is a game of irritations, and I can't have one of our referees being the cause of it.'

"That next season, I scouted him in his first game. He did a great job. After the game was over, I went into the dressing room for a chat. 'How did I do?' he asked me.

"I said, 'You're only asking me that because you know you did a good job, aren't you? One game does not a season make—but that was great. Keep it up.'

"The next night I went to his second game, but he didn't know I was there. He was excellent again. And do you know what? In the informal poll of the coaches at the end of that season he ranked number one."

That's also when he accepted an offer to jump to the ABA for a hefty raise in pay. Nucatola did his job too well.

Fully recognizing the importance of quality officiating, the ABA struck a severe blow to the older league when it hired four of the NBA's top officials for the 1969–70 season. Earl Strom, Norm Drucker, John Vanak, and Joe Gushue together represented a lot of playoff assignments and untold experience in working big games; with their departure the level of officiating in the NBA sank to a new low. The league's supervisor of officials at that time was Dolph Schayes, who had plenty of experience as a player and coach, but no officiating experience to anyone's knowledge beyond refereeing an intramural game at NYU or one of his team's scrimmages. Shortly thereafter Commissioner Walter Kennedy hired Nucatola, who was faced with the task of rebuilding an officiating corps that, because of the addition of three new teams, had to be expanded for the 1970–71 season.

The first thing he decided was that the pay and living conditions had to be improved. For years most league officials were paid by the game —and not very much. If an official made ten thousand dollars he was fortunate, and even that amount wasn't enough to put up with the expected abuse. Nucatola had his eye on hiring some top-flight college officials, but in order to do that he had to be able to make it worth their while.

"We had to come up with more money," he says, "if we were to invite and encourage quality people to come into our league. The good college officials were making fifteen and twenty thousand dollars a year between their regular jobs and part-time officiating, so we had to match that. Oh, maybe we'd have gotten some eager young kid with the old money we were offering, but I was looking for instant improvement."

The pay scale was increased gradually. Not too long ago the salary range was from ten to twenty-five thousand dollars. By the start of the 1974–75 season, the range was from seventeen to thirty-seven thousand. There is additional money available on a per-game basis for officiating in the playoffs now. Referees have liberal travel ex-

For no particular reason, referees seem to feel it is necessary to demonstrate the foul they have called.

penses, and the overall quality of living conditions has been improved drastically.

It is still a lonely life. Until Nucatola instituted a policy of teaming two officials for a month or so as a means of improving their continuity and coordination as a pair, the individual official had always traveled and lived alone. His life was even more jumbled than the players' lives, because he never had the luxury of a home stand. A man living in a non-metropolitan area might get home only two or three times during the six-month, 82-game season.

After signing a few highly regarded college referees immediately upon becoming the officiating supervisor, Nucatola turned his attention toward developing his own prospects, just as a baseball team signs a rookie and sends him through its minor league system. His scouts scour the country and the best prospects are invited to rookie camps he runs in the immediate postseason and again during training camp. Then they work in either the Eastern Basketball Association or the Continental Basketball League, a pair of minor leagues whose playing style most closely approximates the rugged nature of NBA play. The recent opening of the International Basketball Association in Europe has given him another avenue by which to train aspiring NBA officials.

Nucatola feels, as do many other officiating experts, that the best way to train for an officiating spot in the NBA is to first become accustomed to the different style of play. Veteran college referees often must break habits acquired in handling their games. It isn't the written rules that create problems in the pros, it's the unwritten ones that lead to difficulty.

For example, all lower levels of basketball—this includes college ball—insist on a minimum of hand contact between ball handler and defender. It's different in the NBA and ABA because "hand-checking" is allowed. The official NBA rules explain what is and isn't permissible in the following, which is an appendage to Rule 12, Section B, personal fouls: "NOTE: A defensive player is permitted to retain tactile contact with his opponent so long as he does not prevent by such contact the offensive player's movement to his desired objective on the floor." Obviously, the legality of a "hand check" is in the eye of the beholder. What one official considers an impediment to progress might differ from another's opinion.

And thus do player-official bickerings begin over the alleged issue of "consistency." Ask any professional player what he wants most out of an official (aside from every call, of course), and the answer most likely will be "consistency. I want him to call 'em the same at both ends of the floor." Translation: "If I get my arm chopped off when I take a jump shot, I want to be able to chop the other guy's arm off when he takes his jump shot."

The major problem, however, is that different officials may be responsible for the conflicting calls, or non-calls. That is one reason why Nucatola's attempt to pair off the same officials night after night makes sense. By learning each other's tendencies and philosophies, they should be able to coordinate their efforts. "I'm not saying we can improve the officiating by fifteen or twenty percent by pairing them off," Nucatola says, "but perhaps six to eight percent. Every little bit helps."

Another ancient dictum that makes it hard for a young official to become adjusted to the way things are done in the pros is the famous old Sid Borgia theory: "No harm, no foul." Again, everyone has his own interpretation of exactly what constitutes "no harm." Some referees have made the mistake of deciding that anything that happens off the ball is not harmful, but nothing could be more disastrous than following that policy. Mayhem begins off the ball, and only by controlling

If all rough players were honest players, "no harm, no foul" could be followed religiously. But everyone has his own interpretation of exactly what constitutes "no harm."

that activity can the game proceed at all normally.

If all rough players were honest players, "no harm, no foul" could be followed religiously. But when a tough player mixes some good old-fashioned brawling with a bit of chicanery and is allowed to get away with it, retaliatory measures are sure to follow. Then things can get nasty.

One of the more rugged players to enter professional basketball in the past 10 years has been Dave Cowens, whom the 76ers once decided would be the middle linebacker and Most Valuable Player on a mythical NBA All-Football team. "He blocks your shot," exclaimed 76er guard Fred Carter, hardly a shrinking violet himself, "and then he dives on top of you." Yet nobody has accused the aggressive Celtic of playing dirty and, actually, he is an easy player to police.

Cowens' own idea of a fun player to compete against is Golden State center Clifford Ray, who used to play for Chicago. One night they were playing in Chicago and they were busy whacking each other. "Hey, you guys," said referee Jake O'Donnell, "take it easy."

"Aw," Cowens shouted back, "we're just having fun." And Ray concurred. Says Cowens of Ray, "Clifford is rough but never dirty."

Richie Powers, the gray-haired Irishman with the baby face, likes to tell of the fierce playoff struggles between Dave DeBusschere of New York and Gus Johnson of Baltimore. Both were outstanding at both ends of the court, and both were very strong men who knew how to throw their weight around. Neither was the type to complain about an occasional elbow from the other, because they both knew there was no danger of submarining, or some such foul tactic, coming from the other.

It's been much the same when other crafty veterans have met in recent years. One night the Kansas City–Omaha Kings and Celtics played, and

It takes years of experience before an official can do his best work in the league. There are so many things to learn, if only because there are so many ball players who spend their waking moments thinking up new tricks.

Don Nelson and Don Kojis (who can best be described as the Muscle Beach Don Nelson) were conducting their own private pants-tugging, shirt-grabbing war in the corner. "We just let them play their own game," Powers laughed later. "They weren't bothering anyone else."

It takes years of experience before an official can do his best work in the league. There are so many things to learn, if only because there are so many ball players who spend a great deal of their waking moments thinking up new tricks. Probably the worst thing that happened to officiating in the past dozen years was an article under Frank Ramsey's by-line that appeared in *Sports Illustrated,* which outlined myriad ways to draw fouls, not all of them legitimate. Ramsey has inspired a generation of basketball "thespians," and it seems there is no end in sight, because every high school and junior high school kid in America has been imitating them.

Drawing the charge used to mean having the courage to step in front of a man driving to the basket and being willing to get run over for the cause. Indeed, there are many players who are skilled at taking a legitimate charge, not the least of which is Chicago's Jerry Sloan, who also happens to be the leading candidate for the award as "best actor" in the league. No player picks up as many charging fouls, correctly or incorrectly, as Sloan, unless it happens to be his backcourt mate, Norm Van Lier. These two players, as well as others, such as Billy Cunningham and Don Nelson, can go down at the blink of an eyelash, sometimes when the rival player is as much as two feet away.

But for every one of these bogus situations, there are two or three more times when the crucial decision involves an evident case of contact. Then the official must decide whether the offense or defense was at fault, and, aside from goaltending, it's the toughest call he has to make.

Falling down without provocation is but one of many tricks the modern player performs. Another is to stumble off the court during the rebound action, making it seem as if the player had been shoved by a rival rebounder. That often earns a loose ball foul call.

Nelson is adept at several maneuvers, as befits his image as a smart forward. If he starts to encounter difficulty while cutting across the lane, he goes into a stumbling act that makes him look like a man on skates for the first time. The referee assumes he was tripped, and Nelson draws the foul. He has often been known to spring himself for a back door play by the simple expedient of giving his defender a healthy shove as a starting impetus. He is exceptionally good, too, at falling down after attempting a long jumper. Whenever a defensive player makes a rush at a shooter, falling down seems to be a good idea. It is a ploy used by many players.

A young official must be aware of all these tricks, not to mention the special traits of the players themselves. By knowing what a player is likely to do in a certain situation (the Van Arsdale brothers, for example, favor a quick stop and a 180-degree spin when they drive the lane), he can prepare himself for collisions before they happen. This is not to say he should either anticipate or predetermine his calls, but it does mean that he can be prepared on occasion.

By concensus, the men who have acquired the most respect and appreciation over the years are Powers and Rudolph. Powers is in his third NBA stint (he began in 1955, but quit twice when personal problems became insurmountable). It is to the betterment of the league, and professional basketball in general, that he has returned, because he is calling them better than ever.

Powers is the workingman's referee. He is tough, but humorous. He runs the game the way a

foreman runs a shop, allowing slight deviations from the norm but reserving the final say for himself. He never fails to see the humor in a situation, and he recognizes that many players have a need to speak their piece and mean no harm in what they say.

He also has a flair for the dramatic, and he was involved in one of the better playoff episodes, involving coach ·versus official. The Celtics were playing a big playoff game in Los Angeles in the Auerbach era, and Red was baiting Richie unmercifully. Finally, Powers reached his breaking point. He took the whistle out of his mouth and rolled it halfway across the floor until it stopped dead right at Red's feet. "You don't deserve good referees!" he announced to the stunned Boston coach.

By virtue of his assured manner and general accuracy, he has the reputation of being the man most people want to see work a big game.

Mendy Rudolph, the dean of NBA officials, has a somewhat contrasting style but equal authority. Rudolph has been calling NBA games since the age of 25, and that was over 20 years ago. He presently holds the title of referees' Chief of Staff, which makes him a slightly more-than-equal officiating partner for another referee.

Whereas Powers is like the Irish cop on the beat, walking down the street with a wisecrack for everyone, Rudolph is like the maitre d' at a plush restaurant. He knows exactly what constitutes a proper game, much like a headwaiter knows the correct forks and proper wines for a meal. When Mendy spots an infraction, the offender is made to feel that somehow he has soiled the linen tablecloth. Then, before making the call, Mendy draws his lips slowly into a somewhat snobbish sneer, which of course is always artfully but broadly demonstrated to the official scorer as well as the crowd.

Such style, though not necessary, makes officiating more interesting. For no particular reason referees seem to feel it is necessary to demonstrate the foul they have just called. It has become a tradition.

Flamboyant officials of today owe their debt to men such as the late Pat Kennedy, who was often described as "purple faced," and who seems to have been the patron of energetic modern officials such as Manny Sokol. There is no doubt that a colorful referee can spice up a dull game (a one-time NBA ref named Jim Gaffney once brought down an otherwise bored house at a college game by announcing, "Forty-two, you're a blanket!"), but some observers object to their intrusion during a game. "People don't pay to see referees" is the usual explanation.

"As far as style goes," says John Nucatola, "I'll use an analogy from my coaching days. I used to tell my players, 'I don't care what shooting style you use if you can make them. But if you're not hitting very often, you'd better do it my way.' Every referee can't emulate Rudolph and Powers. They all have their own personalities, and we don't want to stifle them. If a man has a flair to his personality, like Manny Sokol, to restrict him would mean he couldn't officiate as well. He's got to be himself. But we can't have showboating for its own sake. People pay to see these magnificent athletes, not one of our referees."

Rudolph's style is one of elegance. He is the Fred Astaire of officials. He glides around the court gracefully, and everything he does, from making a call to handing a basketball to a player, is done with precision. Indeed, one of the oft-imitated Rudolph movements by aficionados of the officiating art is the stylish removal of a bead of sweat with the pinky, and the ever-so-slight flick of the wrist that banishes the droplet to the floor.

The only other person whose movements even vaguely parallel Mendy's is his protégé Dar-

Rudolph is like the maitre d' at a plush restaurant. When Mendy spots an infraction, the offender is made to feel that he has soiled the linen.

rell Garretson. Darrell made one of the most courageous calls of the past several years when he decided that Boston's Jo Jo White had been fouled by Buffalo's Bob McAdoo at the buzzer in the sixth game of their 1974 first-round playoff series. Over eighteen thousand Buffalo fans were ready to scream "Off with his head!" as White made a pair of free throws after time had expired, to give the Celtics the series.

The persistent question in professional basketball is why referee-baiting is allowed to continue at its present level. Surely coaches and players could be made to realize that their present deportment only leads to worse, and not better, officiating. Why should there be such a premium on a referee's emotional stability? Isn't the crowd reaction enough of an outside burden to place on a man who, after all, is only trying to do his job?

It's not as though referees of today are mentally weak men who can't be expected to perform their jobs equally well under variant circumstances. Perhaps 20 or 25 years ago, when teams like Minneapolis or Rochester never lost at home (and one reason was the way the games were officiated), there was a serious question about referees' neutrality. But those days are gone, and the home court advantage today has very little to do with the officiating.

The crowds themselves are no longer the problem. The only time they are a factor is when the coaches incite them, so why can't something be done to tone down the coaches?

Okay, coaches, listen up: Isn't it enough that the two officials must keep track of two clocks and the different time counts, spot zone defense infractions, watch for out-of-bounds calls, see if the man with the ball is attacking someone with his free hand, or is being attacked himself, and decide which of the probable two or three simulta-

neous off-the-ball fouls occurring he is going to call, without worrying about being called uncomplimentary names and having his ancestry questioned—an act that almost surely is going to arouse the crowd and turn it, too, against the referee?

Maybe, as Nucatola suggests, the answer is a third official. Perhaps if there was a third pair of eyes scanning the court, players would stop some of the things they are presently doing, realizing they couldn't get away with them. Certain college conferences have already experimented with a third official, and the NBA itself has tried it during a couple of exhibition seasons, but the reviews have been lukewarm.

As usual, no matter what the officials do, they wind up as villains. If they call a very tight game, coaches and players moan, "Aw, let 'em play." If they try to avoid a foul line parade by "letting 'em play," the cry invariably is, "They were lettin' 'em get away with murder!"

The truth is that officiating, and the game itself, could be improved if it weren't the "American way" to always try for the upper hand. If deceit, chicanery, trickery, and simple dishonesty in the form of a thousand and one illegal maneuvers preferred by the game's top players were eliminated, and if coaches were muzzled for the two hours it takes to play a game, officiating would be a nice way to make a living. After all, like writers, officials get paid for watching excellent basketball.

As it is, however, the perfect official would have to have the self-assurance of Kojak, the sense of humor of Woody Allen, the wisdom of Solomon, and the job security of a Supreme Court Justice. It shouldn't have to be that way, but that's the reality of the situation. After all, the game couldn't exist without them. "Call referees necessary evils if you will," points out John Nucatola, "but they *are* necessary."

The perfect official would have to have the self-assurance of Kojak, the sense of humor of Woody Allen, the security of a Supreme Court Justice.

The Ultimate Weapon

3

Centers

The man who first called the center on a basketball team the "pivotman" affixed a most descriptive name to this demanding position. On a professional level, teams seldom progress far without a standout center.

The center is truly the pivot, or central figure, both offensively and defensively, on most teams. A great center can carry an otherwise inferior team to the NBA finals, as Kareem Abdul-Jabbar did in 1973. So crippled was the team at various stages of the 1973–74 season, that one observer referred to the Milwaukee Bucks as "Kareem and four waver wires." Yet, as long as the 7-foot 3-inch star remained in the lineup, the Bucks continued to win.

The reverse is likewise true. There have always been professional basketball teams with ideal supporting casts that lacked a quality center. The pre-Bill Russell Celtics, for instance, had Bob Cousy, Bill Sharman, and Ed Macauley, and were constant playoff threats. They were never champions, however, because the skinny McCauley was not a true center and couldn't do the things a great center must do. It was only when the Celtics acquired Russell that they reached their full potential.

Throughout league history teams have lost in championship play because they lacked a superior center. The long string of Celtic titles might very well have been interrupted on any one of several occasions had the Los Angeles Lakers possessed a better center to tangle with Russell. Ray Felix, Larry Foust, Jim Krebs, Leroy Ellis, Gene Wiley, and Darrall Imhoff were all willing work-

ers, men who continually put forth their best effort, but none was a serious threat to Russell's game-by-game dominance. Though the Lakers had Elgin Baylor and Jerry West playing together several years at peak, or near-peak, efficiency, and though their other starting forward was the underrated Rudy LaRusso, they never defeated Boston when they had to, and the difference was usually Russell.

In the past quarter century of professional basketball, the closest any NBA team has come to winning without a top-flight center was when, in 1973, the New York Knicks defeated the Lakers in the finals with a 70-percent-effective Willis Reed.

The public generally associates the center with offense, a way of thinking that starts in high school, progresses through college, and quite naturally continues on to the professional level. The classic image of a center is that of a Chamberlain scoring 100 points or averaging 50.4 points a game, as he did in 1961–62. In other words, people tend not to think in terms of a center's total offense, but of his individual scoring.

The fact is, however, that a professional center's most important job is defense. An auxiliary assignment is to rebound, for the simple fact is that it is impossible to play without the basketball. For most centers scoring is a bonus.

Regardless of the style of play preferred by a center, a team must revolve around him. Thus, Abdul-Jabbar's team and Bob Lanier's Detroit team both begin an inordinate number of offenses by getting the ball to their centers. It makes sense. Both men are superior shooters, and they have a better chance of making one of their pet shots

than any of their teammates do of making theirs.

The Celtics' offense has always been based on the center position. Though Russell is best remembered as a great rebounder and shot blocker, he was also an excellent offensive center (which is not to be confused with the ability to score). He had an excellent understanding of team offense and was constantly aware of the play around him. He could pass, set picks, and maneuver subtly to make the Boston offense function smoothly.

When Dave Cowens became the Boston center two years after Russell retired, the Celtics incorporated plays and offensive sets into their offense to take advantage of his superior scoring ability. At the same time, they continued to run plays as though Russell was still there. Cowens, though he contributed more points personally to the offense, did not immediately understand the system that was set up to enable others to score as well, despite the fact that he is unselfish and a better-than-average passer.

Offensively, Abdul-Jabbar is the greatest force ever to play the game. Chamberlain backers will argue that Wilt's feats (100 points in one game, an average of 50.4 points a game for an entire season, 4,029 points in one season) are testimony to his superiority, but it must be remembered that Abdul-Jabbar would never take that many shots. Nobody yet knows what this gifted man's peak output would be if he simply dedicated himself to scoring points.

What makes Abdul-Jabbar so devastating on offense is the completeness of his game. In addition to being the closest thing to an automatic two points as exists in the game, he is also a skilled passer. To play him one-on-one is to invite a good shot, but to double or triple-team him is to invite a better shot for someone else.

Jabbar's suspected value to a team was confirmed at the beginning of the 1974–75 season,

**Playing without Abdul-Jabbar for the
first five weeks of the season,
Milwaukee saw its shooting percentage
drop to next-to-last place.**

93

when he was forced to miss games because of a broken bone in his hand. For the preceding five seasons, the Bucks had led the league in field goal percentage. In 1970–71, they became the first professional team ever to make over half its attempted shots (.509). Playing without Abdul-Jabbar for the first five weeks of the season, Milwaukee saw its shooting percentage drop to next-to-last place in the league, ahead only of expansion New Orleans. Then consider that in the year prior to Abdul-Jabbar's arrival (as Lew Alcindor), the Bucks finished in a tie for twelfth among 14 teams in the matter of shooting percentage. Obviously, Kareem made the difference.

Because Abdul-Jabbar is over 7 feet 2 inches tall, many detractors of the sport assume that his size is the major reason for his success. Basketball's critics have said that about every big man who has enjoyed even modest success, beginning with the 6-foot "goons" of the Naismith era (the doctor assumed that nobody could possibly touch a rim 10 feet above the ground); continuing through players of the twenties, such as Joe Lapchick (6-5); right up to modern players such as Mikan, Bob Kurland, Russell, and Chamberlain.

The important factor in professional basketball today, and this includes the forward and guard positions as well, is not how big you are but how big you play. Jumping ability and muscle do a lot to counteract a lack of height and therefore a Dave Cowens, who is 6 feet 8½ inches, can play center at the highest level because he can jump, run, and throw elbows as well as anyone. Westley Unseld, by virtue of his girth ("He sets a pick," says one rival, "and it takes you twenty-four seconds to run around it") and excellent lateral mobility—when he isn't battling knee problems—also plays center well, despite the fact that he is barely 6 feet 6½ inches tall.

Hank Finkel, on the other hand, is 7 feet tall

but plays at approximately a 6-foot 8-inch level because he cannot jump well and has poor lateral mobility. Size alone is simply not enough to guarantee success although, admittedly, it is often enough to guarantee a player a job. Finkel would never have played were he 2 inches shorter. Chop Abdul-Jabbar down to 6 feet 1 inch, however, and you'd have an excellent guard.

Other than the simple physical and physiological abilities of coordination, strength, and timing, there is an aptitude for a given sport that a prospective athlete must possess if he is to excel. It is true of any basketball player, even the big men, and it is more than an injustice to label them as freaks. Again, Russell Sherman can throw light on the matter:

"One sport, for instance, that a solo performer can identify with is golf. It's a game of you versus yourself. It requires a high degree of versatility and adaptability.

"The point is that Bob Rosburg and Julius Boros are no less athletes because they can't run around the reservoir in less than six minutes. I think there is in every sport one element featured above all the others that represents the expertise of that particular sport. To be able to do that, I think, is astonishing and supernormal. You're not supernormal just because you are six-six or seven feet tall. I don't think that six-six or seven feet means you're a basketball player either."

There is, for instance, the much-discussed, but seldom analyzed matter of the dunk. Chamberlain's point totals were widely maligned because he dunked so many shots. Now, there are dunks and there are dunks. Some dunks are the result of pure circumstance. The man gets an uncontested offensive rebound, for instance, and he jams it through. Perhaps he has been basket-hanging and he winds up with a wide-open shot after a steal or quick turnover. Those dunks reflect nothing more than size or jumping skill. Some of Wilt's dunks fit that mold, but others were the result of his backing his man so far underneath the basket that he had the opportunity to dunk. Within the framework of basketball, this represents skill. Some Chamberlain dunks were awesome because they came in traffic. Others were the result of good offensive movement that put him in a position to accept a good pass.

Lacking Chamberlain's raw physical power, Abdul-Jabbar cannot bull his way in to get the dunks that Wilt used to get. He has a better-rounded offensive game but will never accumulate comparable scoring totals (another reason being the different team concept under which he plays). Yet he is taller than all but one man (Seattle's young Tommy Burleson) in his league, and he probably has been the tallest man in professional basketball for the past five years. Were he 6 feet 11 inches tall, or even 6 feet 9 inches, he would still be a great offensive center. And if he couldn't shoot sweeping hooks and artfully executed turnarounds from distances up to 18 feet, he wouldn't be half the scorer he is.

Kareem can be considered the classic back-to-the-basket pivotman on offense. His favorite weapon is a graceful right-handed hook, which in Milwaukee has been nicknamed the "sky hook." Few opponents have ever gotten a hand on the shot (Cowens, who is about 7 inches shorter, is one of the lucky ones). Chamberlain, for some unknown reason, never developed a hook, although in his early and middle years he liked to wheel inside in a hook-like manner to dunk the ball.

In basketball today, Abdul-Jabbar has the best hook. His range is absolutely phenomenal, and what really makes him dangerous is the fact that he can sink the shot from the corner. Most basketball players will agree that the toughest basic shot is the corner hook, and only Jerry Lucas

The important factor in professional basketball today, and this includes the forward and guard positions as well, is not how big you are but how big you play.

among Abdul-Jabbar's contemporaries has tried one often. Surely, anyone who saw the gorgeous right corner hook the big man swished to win the sixth game of the 1974 playoff finals against Boston is aware of the potency of the shot.

The major flaw preventing Abdul-Jabbar from being called the ultimate inside weapon is his lack of a left hand. There was a time when he dabbled with a left hook, but he quickly abandoned the move. Since most teams ask their center to overplay Kareem toward his right hand, he would pose an impossible problem if he ever came up with a suitable left-handed shot.

Centers can be divided into two offensive categories, the Chamberlain–Abdul-Jabbar inside type or the Cowens–Bob McAdoo outside type. Naturally there are always hybrids, such as Nate Thurmond, who has a strong inside game and an erratic outside game. Cowens is perhaps as versatile as it is possible to be; he possesses an overpowering inside game against men his size or a little bigger and a strong outside game when he plays monsters such as Abdul-Jabbar.

George Mikan effectively set the tone for modern pivot play with his hook shots and inside power lay-ups. Chamberlain refined the power game and added an effective fall-away jumper. The shot was apparently an ego trip—all his coaches felt it was ridiculous for him to take any shot in which his follow-through would carry him away from the basket. Wilt stubbornly insisted on using the move in his prime years, if for no other reason than to prove he didn't rely on his size and strength to score points.

Though Cowens is generally seen as the forerunner of the so-called "new breed" of mobile, outside-shooting centers, he too had spiritual antecedents in the 24-second era, dating back to Ed McCauley, who was an esteemed-enough Celtic in pre-Russell days to have had his number re-tired by the club. Macauley was an outside shooter who frustrated bigger and stronger foes such as Mikan with his long shots.

Another excellent shooter for a big man was Clyde Lovellette, whose soft touch belied his bulk—which was considerable. Lovellette was an unstoppable scorer for the Minneapolis Lakers, Cincinnati Royals, St. Louis Hawks, and last, the Celtics, where he backed up Russell and was dubbed "Wide Clyde" by Boston announcer Johnny Most. Lovellette favored a soft one-handed set, a shot that is nearly extinct today.

As the game progressed into the sixties, more centers began to hit outside shots. Walt Bellamy was extremely proficient from the foul line area with a jumper, as was Zelmo Beaty. But 15 feet remained the maximum range of a center until Willis Reed and Elvin Hayes came along.

Reed spent a great deal of his early career with New York as a forward, where, though miscast, he nevertheless made a strong impression. As a forward he developed his shooting range to about 20 feet, giving him an edge on most rival centers when the 1968 trade of Bellamy gave him the starting pivot job.

At 6 feet 9 inches and 240 pounds, Reed was strong. He was also quick—his success as a forward proved that. He developed the full range of offensive center play. In fact, no center today can match his variety of deft inside moves, and not many shoot as well from the outside. He also aided the New York offense with his passing and pick-setting.

Elvin Hayes came into the NBA in the 1968–69 season and immediately made an impression. He led the league in scoring as a rookie, doing much of his shooting from the outside, though he was a center for the San Diego Rockets.

Almost as impressive as Hayes's volume of shots was his range. "He keeps going out farther and farther,'' marveled Reed one night. ''I can't believe it.'' A great percentage of Elvin's shots were from over 15 feet, many of those from more than 20.

Even though big men had long since established the fact that their scoring could come from anywhere, the professional basketball world was hardly prepared for Cowens when he joined the Celtics in 1970. He was a new type of center.

Shooting from the outside was only part of it. He was also fast enough up and down the floor to participate in the fast break. Russell had generally been content to get the defensive rebound, pitching the ball out quickly to start the break, then standing in place to admire the play. Occasionally he got into the act as a late trailer and wound up with a convenient stuff shot, the result of a Cousy pass. Most of the time, however, he lagged back until he could determine whether or not the fast break had broken down.

Cowens, however, was not one to stand around. He got the ball, pitched it out, then filled a lane in hopes of getting the shot himself or creating an opening for someone else. He didn't have to be a wing man on the break to cause trouble, either. He was, and is, a potent force as a trailer, getting a delayed fast break pass at the top of the key and making an unmolested jumper. Veteran observers were astounded. Even the thought of a center starting a fast break with a defensive rebound, then finishing it with a driving lay-up, was something new.

The value of a center with an outside shot is enormous. Big centers are, by nature and training, unwilling voyagers into the ''outside world.'' They are taught to stay close to the basket to ''clog up the middle,'' à la Russell, and to grab as many defensive rebounds as they can. Obviously, a shooting center who is left unguarded outside poses a tremendous threat to the defense.

Some of Wilt's dunks reflect nothing more than size or jumping skill, but others are the result of his backing his man far under the basket to get the chance.

Once a man has done no more than establish his ability to connect from the outside, he has already helped his team. If he is played tightly by his counterpart, various other offensive options are open. A vivid example occurred in the first game of the 1974 playoff finals between Boston and Milwaukee. Abdul-Jabbar, with four years of experience in playing Dave Cowens at his disposal, chose to vacate his favored spot beneath the basket and, instead, played Cowens tightly outside. Boston immediately started running plays designed to take advantage of Abdul-Jabbar's absence from the middle. The irony is that Abdul-Jabbar hadn't even waited to see if Cowens would hit from the outside. He went right after him. The Celtics had confidence in their other players and in their set offense, so the fact that Cowens was being covered from the outside didn't upset them. Kareem was paying Cowens a supreme compliment by abandoning the nest in order to guard him, and the Celtics said thanks by taking a 95–83 triumph that was nowhere near that close a ball game.

Cowens himself knew the feeling of being drawn away from the basket by a great-shooting outside center, because he had been similarly teased in the 1972 playoffs by Jerry Lucas, the most amazing long-range shooting center of them all. Lucas had a weird release on his favorite shot, letting it go in shot-put style from shoulder level while propelling himself in a scissors kick. It was a unique shot, and Lucas was able to hit from 30 feet away if need be.

One of the most heralded college players of all time while at Ohio State, Lucas had spent the majority of his career as a forward and was known primarily as a skilled position rebounder. He bounced from Cincinnati to Golden State (San Francisco, if you will) and finally to New York, where his career took a dramatic turn. Willis Reed

began experiencing physical difficulties, which limited his playing time, and Lucas, who was barely 6 feet 8 inches tall, was shifted to center. The Knicks immediately had the most outside-shooting-oriented offense ever seen, with all five starters capable of hitting 20-footers, and with the center and one forward (Dave DeBusschere) having a greater range on their shots than either of the starting guards.

With Lucas alternately infuriating or amazing rival centers, New York finished second in the regular season race behind Boston, won the Eastern Conference playoff title (beating the Celtics in five games), and went all the way to the finals before bowing to the potent Lakers.

Without prior warning, there emerged on the scene in the fall of 1973 a shooter who was so incredibly accurate that league personnel exhausted themselves searching for proper adjectives. Bob McAdoo had won a lukewarm race for Rookie of the Year while playing forward the year before, so no one had an inkling that he would enjoy a spectacular 1973–74 season as a center who would win both the scoring and field goal percentage titles in the same year, an unprecedented feat.

McAdoo demonstrated a varied offensive game. Unlike Hayes, who is mechanical with his ceaseless barrage of turnaround jumpers, McAdoo proved he could score in many ways. His calling card, however, was a jump shot that had no set spot or distance. Whether left wide open or covered by two men, McAdoo continually glided upward and got off a gorgeous shot. No less an astute (or conservative) evaluator of basketball talent than John Havlicek candidly admitted that McAdoo was the greatest outside shooter he had seen in 12 years of professional basketball.

Ironically, McAdoo became the Buffalo center by accident rather than by design. The chain of events began when general manager Eddie

Elvin Hayes came into the NBA and immediately made an impression. He led the league in scoring as a rookie. Almost as impressive as Hayes's volume of shots was his range.

Donovan, anxious to find a quality "small" forward for his team, traded his incumbent center, Elmore Smith, to Los Angeles for Jim McMillian. The team's original assumption was that a rugged 6-foot 8-inch center-forward named Bob Kauffman, who had played an acceptable center for the team the year before Smith was drafted, would again play center, and that McAdoo would remain at forward. Kauffman, however, had a physical problem, a hip alignment condition that had been first diagnosed as a severe groin pull. McAdoo was hastily shifted to center until Kauffman was well enough to return to the lineup. It turned out to be basketball's answer to the Wally Pipp headache that kicked off Lou Gehrig's 2,130 consecutive-game streak for the Yankees.

What McAdoo and Cowens brought to the position that few people felt either could play was quickness. Each man has superior running speed as well as exceptional lateral mobility. Each is a great jumper. Each has marvelous instincts for the game. "I have always contended," said Bob Cousy, "that basketball is not a game of height and muscle, but rather one of speed and quick-ness." Cowens and McAdoo were offered as proof. Though each man stands no taller than 6 feet 9 inches, each man *plays* somewhere around 7 feet 2 inches, and with a quickness and pace that no 7-footer can match. The major difference between the two is Cowens' muscle, which he often uses to great advantage when he plays McAdoo.

Though offense is the first thing that generally comes to mind when people think of centers, the fact remains that defense is more important. Knowing that 10 shooters can be found by shaking a tree anywhere in the country, professional scouts are forever searching for mobile centers who can get the ball and somehow prevent the other team from putting it back into the basket.

"The center is the quarterback of the defense," explains Cowens, who has always enjoyed playing defense more than shooting the basketball. "He must see everything that's happening, call out the picks, and be ready to help out if somebody else's man gets through." An even clearer analogy might be that the center is basketball's answer to a baseball team's catcher for defensive

purposes—the entire game is in front of him.

There are many facets to a center's defensive play (Bill Russell is perhaps the only one to have effectively mastered them all). Primarily, defense is thought of in terms of blocking shots. Blocked shots have a place in basketball, of course, but they are overrated as a criterion for evaluating the defensive ability of a center. For one thing, blocked shots are not necessarily useful if a man swats the ball out of bounds. Russell, who pioneered the art of blocking shots, and who had a more profound impact on the way the game is played today than anyone else, recognized early in his career that if a blocked shot was good, then a blocked shot that could start a fast break was even better. Most players are pleased if they merely block an opponent's shot; few have the coordination or determination required to learn how to *direct* the blocked shot to where it will do the most good. Today, the best practitioner of the art is Nate Thurmond. Cowens is good at directing, but he seldom blocks a shot.

There is also the matter of the number of blocked shots. No statistics were kept on the num-

"I have always contended," said Bob Cousy, "that basketball is not a game of height and muscle, but rather one of speed and quickness." 101

ber of shots blocked by Russell and Chamberlain during their careers, but one safe assumption is that the total was far short of what they could have blocked had they chosen to do so. Russell, in particular, had a marvelous psychological and cerebral approach to the game. His opponents, realizing that he could block virtually any one of their shots, were so afraid of him that their concentration would be ruined anyway. They'd miss shots they could have made, and in Russell's book those misses were as good as blocked shots. In the last minute or two of play, however, with the game on the line, Russell would take no chances of a lucky shot going in, and he'd do some serious rejecting.

Some of the modern shot blockers, such as Elmore Smith, plus Artis Gilmore and Caldwell Jones of the ABA, do not have Russell's mental approach to the game. Smith, for instance, is so enamored of the blocked shot that he will try for anything. The media feed his shot-blocking hunger by making a fuss over achievements such as 17 alleged blocked shots in one game and his winning the championship in blocked shots. The NBA followed the ABA's lead and instituted the blocked shot as an official statistic for the 1973–74 season. Insiders know that the statistic, like many other stats, is essentially meaningless.

The center who is preoccupied with the blocked shot at the expense of his other responsibilities is almost certain to be a profound defensive liability in the long run. Such players have a tendency to jump every time the ball is near them. They can then be up-faked and driven past, which creates easy scoring situations. They also are prone to foul trouble (Smith has always had this problem, which isn't surprising). The value of having an effective inside deterrent should not be understated. Intimidators certainly have their place, but discriminating intimidators have even more of a place.

All good teams have a concept of team defense distinct from and above the five individual man-to-man scenarios that are taking place. The ultimate worth of a center, or any other player on defense, is how well he augments the team defensive concept. The Celtics, when they are of a mind to do so and when they have all their horses, play an extremely aggressive pressure defense, placing a premium on switching, lateral mobility, and instant reaction. If a team is intent on switching, the most important asset they can possess is a center who will not be embarrassed when he is matched up with guards or forwards. When the center is Dave Cowens, it is often the guards and forwards who wind up looking silly.

Cowens' willingness and, more importantly, his ability to switch onto dangerous corner and backcourt scoring threats makes the entire Boston defensive concept possible. Much has been said and written about his unique function in their defense, but one fabulous play he executed in the 1974 playoffs furnished a devastating example.

It was the historic sixth game of the final series with Milwaukee. A Celtic victory would make them world champions for the twelfth time, but they had spent most of the game (on their home floor) trailing Abdul-Jabbar and the Bucks. Milwaukee had an 84–78 lead with 2:35 remaining in regulation play, but Boston fought back and finally tied the score at 86–86 on a right corner jumper by Cowens with 1:06 to play. Milwaukee called time out. When play resumed, the Bucks worked the ball around unsuccessfully until, with 9 seconds remaining on the 24-second clock, Cowens switched off to guard Oscar Robertson, the consummate ball handler and experienced floor leader. In doing so, Cowens risked the possibility of some kind of lob pass to Abdul-Jabbar on the inside, but neither he nor the Celtics cared about that.

Though offense is the first thing that generally comes to mind when people think of centers, the fact remains that defense is more important. "The center is the quarterback of the defense."

Now it was Robertson versus Cowens, the clever 6-foot 5-inch guard against the aggressive 6-foot 9-inch center. Cowens was all over Oscar, waving his arms wildly to prevent the veteran from seeing anything else on the floor. Forget the lob pass. The Bucks would have been satisfied to get off any kind of a shot.

Finally, Cowens reached out and knocked the ball away from Robertson. It rolled toward midcourt, seemingly heading out of bounds at the intersection of the midcourt line and the sideline. That in itself would have been a great play because, though the ball would have belonged to Milwaukee, they would then have had only a few seconds to work for a shot.

Cowens was not content to let it rest there. He treated the 15,320 fans in the Boston Garden and the 38.9 million who viewed the game on television to the inspiring sight of a reckless 6-foot 9-inch, 230 pound, redheaded madman belly flopping onto the floor and skidding some eight feet on his stomach in vigorous pursuit of the ball. It was something not to be easily forgotten by those who saw it.

The first reaction was that Cowens had created a jump ball situation with Robertson. But referee Don Murphy, a third official seated on the sideline to handle clock situations such as this one, correctly ruled that while Cowens was outhustling Robertson for the ball, the 24-second clock had expired. The ball belonged to Boston.

Whenever coaches in the future discuss the role of a center in team defense, that play will be cited. That Cowens was capable of making the play probably came as no surprise to those who knew him best, however. Both friends and foes of the Florida State product can easily recall the sight of Cowens playing the point on the Seminoles' full-court press.

Since few centers could hope to emulate

Since few centers could hope to emulate
Cowens' approach—even if they possessed
his intensity—they must bring different
assets to their teams' defenses.

Cowens' approach—even if they possessed his intensity—the others must bring different assets to their respective teams' defenses. The primary skill that a center who is not a Dave Cowens can bring to his job is the ability to "cover," or "help out." Covering could mean blocking a shot, or it could simply mean getting in somebody's way just enough to disturb a shot or to ruin a play. Many centers are good at protecting the basket.

Unfortunately, many are inept when it comes to the final phase of defense—man-to-man guarding. Straight-up defense, as it is called, involves concentration, determination, intelligence, and experience. It requires the keeping of a mental book on each rival, listing his likes and dislikes on the floor. Is he left- or right-handed? Can he use his other hand? Which shot in his repertoire does he use from which spot on the floor? How much contact does he like? Does he follow his shots well? How aware is he of his teammates' actions on the floor? If left to double-team someone, is he likely to cut immediately for the basket, or will he just stand and watch the action? Is there a rhythm to his shooting? Does he employ head and shoulder fakes, or should one go up with him as soon as he appears ready to shoot? The good defensive center must always be thinking.

Since Russell retired in 1969, the most heralded straight-up defensive center has been Nate Thurmond of the San Francisco Golden State Warriors and Chicago Bulls. Though NBA people have long recognized his defensive excellence, his reputation in the public eye was acquired only after Abdul-Jabbar stated that the toughest man he had had to face was Thurmond. Inasmuch as Wilt Chamberlain was still active, as was Willis Reed, the opinion surprised some people.

As if to fully demonstrate to Abdul-Jabbar and the basketball public at large just how accurate the contention was, Thurmond startled people by doing a fantastic defensive job on the Milwaukee scoring machine in the 1973 playoff series between the Warriors and the Bucks. By continually beating Abdul-Jabbar to his favorite spots on the floor (cutting down the angles is a big part of defense) and working constantly, the 6-foot 11-inch Thurmond held Abdul-Jabbar to an unheard of 42 percent shooting percentage from the floor (he usually shoots about 53 percent) as Golden State won the series in six games.

Thurmond's style is hardly flamboyant. He blocks shots, but not in the same quantity as Russell or Chamberlain. He is capable of switching off, à la Cowens, but he doesn't favor this tactic, most likely because his aim is to fit into his team's defensive concept. He probably does play the best straight-up defense of all the centers, and he protects the basket extremely well. He is a solid, honest worker on defense, and it pays off.

Chamberlain was capable of great feats defensively, but the bulk of his contributions consisted of clogging the middle and risking goaltending with some near-outrageous blocks. He certainly was not agile enough to jump-switch in Cowens' fashion, and some said the number of memorable hustling plays he made in his 14-year career (1959–1973) was equal to the number of outdoor skating rinks in Saudi Arabia.

Abdul-Jabbar plays aggressive defense in spurts. At such times, he is a devastating force because he does possess above-average quickness. His defensive play, as well as his rebounding, however, is often marked by a curious passiveness.

Artis Gilmore is widely regarded as the most imposing defensive obstacle in the history of the ABA. He specializes in blocked shots, but he can be burned by an outside shooter who is capable of thinking on the court. Such a man is the clever New York Nets' center, Bill Paultz, who always

Straight-up defense involves concentration, determination, intelligence, and experience. It requires the keeping of a mental book on each rival.

seems to combat Gilmore effectively in playoff games.

Rebounding has been called an adjunct to defense, and it certainly is a prerequisite for any center aspiring to greatness. If a meal without wine is like a day without sunshine, as proponents of the grape suggest, then a center without rebounding skill is like a hit man without a gun.

Statistics will reveal that the two greatest rebounders were Russell and Chamberlain, which should come as no surprise. Wilt finished with more rebounds by the end of his career, but it was generally agreed that Russell got more clutch and difficult-to-get rebounds.

When the center gets a rebound is more important than how often he gets one. Some players make a point of getting easy rebounds in order to pad their statistics and yet never seem to get an important rebound when the team needs it. Beware of the player who out-fights his own teammate for the rebound of a missed foul shot, the easiest rebound of all. The defensive team is given the inside position and, unless there is a particularly long rebound, it is very difficult for the defense *not* to get it. The truly great rebounders get rebounds that are timely and difficult to reach. Scouts always inquire about a young big man: "Does he rebound well in traffic, or does he get his rebounds when nobody else is around?"

Teams that execute the fundamentals of rebounding, such as blocking opponents out from a rebounding position, will come up with at least a commensurate share of rebounds. Such a team was the 1969–70 Boston Celtics, the first Celtic team in 13 years to play without the comforting presence of Bill Russell. They hustled and accumulated decent enough team rebounding totals, but they lost several games because of their inability to come up with the key rebound at the crucial part of the game. Russell nearly always

provided that service for them, just as Cowens was to do when he joined the team a year later.

The underneath battle for positioning and, eventually, for the ball itself is a brutal war and one that makes the tag "noncontact" in reference to basketball nonsensical. The variety of activities that takes place in its backboard jungle includes elbowing, punching, holding, pushing, and outright tackling. It is a rough world. Jumping is a useful asset, but it is useless, per se, unless the man has timing to go along with it. In most cases, there is only one exact moment to go up for the ball. An incorrect judgment, either a split second too soon or too late, will almost invariably result in a missed rebound in traffic. Some of the game's great leapers are only mediocre rebounders.

Rebounding is an intricate art, offensive rebounding a specialized art. For reasons to do with geography and rebounding angles, more forwards come up with offensive rebounds than centers, a fact of basketball life little understood by most fans. Centers generally earn their rebounding bread by getting the ball from the defensive backboard and on the offensive end by simply getting a hand in to keep the ball alive.

It has always been difficult to determine exactly what is legal and what is not legal in acquiring a rebounding position under the boards. There is often such an excessive amount of bumping, pushing, and shoving that it seems as though anything goes. About the only thing that, if detected, does not go is for a man in back of an opponent to place his hand on his rival's shoulder and use it as a launching pad. The major problem is that when a man does get a rebound over the head of one who has an inside position, a referee often assumes that he *did* obtain it illegally even if he didn't.

The least developed skill among centers is passing. Most centers can hand the ball off to a man cutting by them, but few centers have ever been superior passers, men who could be inventive, not just reactionary, on the floor.

Perhaps the best passing center who ever played was John "Red" Kerr, a friendly man who played for what seemed like half a century for the Syracuse Nationals and Baltimore Bullets. The 6-foot 10-inch Kerr was always a threat to hit a cutting teammate with a behind-the-back or between-the-legs pass, and he could make plays better than most guards. Russell was another good passer, but he didn't have Kerr's flair.

Chamberlain went at passing the way he did everything else—except for those two great years in Philadelphia from 1966 to 1968—which is to say it was all or nothing. In his early days he thought a pass was something you directed at a waitress. By the end of his career he did nothing but pass. He, too, favored the fancy pass if at all possible, and he became quite adept at a blind backwards bounce pass for a man going back door. He remains the only center ever to lead the league in assists (8.6 a game in 1967–68), but he concentrated so much on passing that he rendered the feat less meaningful than it would have been otherwise.

Lucas, who was essentially a forward, was another outstanding passer.

Surprisingly, considering his bulk and the general plodding nature of his play, one of today's best passing centers is Tom Boerwinkle of Chicago. At 7 feet and 265 pounds, he looks like a hulking misfit left over from football tryout camp but, under coach Dick Motta, he has played a major role in the success of Chicago's patterned offense. He has excellent peripheral vision, as well as command of all types of passes. He also sets a gargantuan pick.

Abdul-Jabbar can also destroy defenses with his passing. He is, by now, so used to double-teaming that the process is fairly simple for him. He spots the open man quickly and he passes the ball crisply. Being 7 feet 3 inches tall hasn't hurt him either. He sees what's happening on the floor as clearly as if he were sitting in the front row of the balcony. He makes some amazing passes from corner to corner to a free teammate simply by lobbing the ball over everyone's head.

Cowens, too, is an above-average passing center. He, of course, is so agile that the ability to pass flows naturally from his basic style of play. He probably excels all the current centers at passing on the move. He makes some of his best passes as part of a fast break group of, say, three-on-one or four-on-two.

In general, however, coaches consider passing ability superfluous to a center's real function. Only in an offense such as Boston's or Chicago's, where many of the plays involve people cutting off a post man, or on a team with Abdul-Jabbar, whose forte is short and middle distance shooting and passing, is it even an issue. Most teams don't worry about their center's ability to pass. But centers who can pass—men like Boerwinkle, Abdul-Jabbar, and Bill Walton—do enhance a team's offense.

In professional basketball today there are talented centers of dramatically contrasted styles, which means that on a great many nights a fan can observe some fascinating battles. There are, for example, the super big men, all of whom have different skills. Abdul-Jabbar possesses the unstoppable hook shot and the semi-unstoppable turnaround jumper. Bob Lanier has a more varied offensive game. He, too, has a hook; it is a very accurate one and he can do a lot more facing the basket than Abdul-Jabbar can. He has a better jump shot and he has far more range. He also can go to the basket with dexterity and authority. In fact, in many ways he is the ultimate in big-man offense. He is certainly one of the most enjoyable players to watch.

Lanier is 6 feet 11 inches tall and weighs (when he's in shape) 250 pounds. Reportedly he wears a size 22 sneaker. In other words, he is one big hombre. Yet he has such exquisite grace that the only proper nickname for him is the "Ballerina Elephant." No big man in the history of the sport has ever brought such agility and such a soft shooting touch to the game.

At one point in Lanier's NBA career with the Detroit Pistons, he was indifferent about rebounding and defense. He was a scorer from the first day he walked into the league (having one bad knee at the time), but it took a while for his total game to be put together. It is now.

Kentucky's Artis Gilmore reigns supreme in the ABA. The goateed 7-foot 2-inch Jacksonville product has probably been held back by playing in the ABA instead of the more polished NBA, but in at least one category he has it all over Abdul-Jabbar and Lanier. He is a rebounding and shot-blocking man. His offense continues to improve. He was a late bloomer as a ball player, and only after joining the professional ranks was he properly taught how to make use of his agility and size. He has worked on his hook shot to the point where no opponent is anxious to see him crank up for one.

Cowens and McAdoo are completely different centers. Cowens is a versatile center whose repertoire includes the ability to shoot from the outside. McAdoo is a phenomenal shooter, a good rebounder, and a good shot blocker. McAdoo plays in the same manner against Cowens as he does against Abdul-Jabbar. Cowens, on the other hand, varies his approach according to the competition.

McAdoo's style bespeaks an effortlessness and grace that reduces the game to certain basics. He glides around the court until he receives the

Kareem's job on the team is not the same as Bill's. Each job differs because it reflects not only the skills of the men's teammates but their own strengths.

ball. Only rarely does he advance it by dribbling; rather, he bounces it once and rises, almost levitates, until, at the peak of his jump, he flips the ball toward the basket. He does not have a great variety of moves, although he can drive past a defender whom he has faked into the air. The overwhelming majority of his baskets come as a result of his unmatched jump shot.

Cowens, conversely, is intense, almost reckless on the court. He plays every game as if it meant reprieve from a life sentence at hard labor. He is more physically explosive than McAdoo. When he *really* wants a rebound, he rockets into the air and attacks the ball. Though he is coordinated and fluid, there is always the suspicion that he is only partially under control. He is a creature of emotion, almost mercurial, which accounts for the frightening stretches of raw power he displays on the court. He has a temper, too, that shows in moments of stress. Indeed, it is only since he has learned to curb his temper somewhat that he has reached his potential as a ball player.

When McAdoo plays against Abdul-Jabbar, there is a David versus Goliath tinge to the proceedings. The slender marksman teases the giant with his outside shooting. If he succeeds in luring Kareem away from the basket, he may attempt an occasional drive. Even though much of Cowens' success against Abdul-Jabbar stems from his own outside shooting, he accomplishes enough on a physical level inside to at least suggest that the match-up is one of a small giant versus a large giant—if that is possible.

Though McAdoo is as swift as any center today, it is Cowens who succeeds in making a confrontation with Milwaukee's intimidating giant a battle of attrition. McAdoo may be as fast a runner as Cowens, but he doesn't exert the constant mental pressure on the big men that Cowens does. Cowens runs from endline to endline for 48 min-

utes, and more than once the Celtics have defeated a Lanier- or Abdul-Jabbar-led team because Cowens was running in the last 5 minutes and the bigger man was lagging behind.

Thurmond provides an interesting evening's work for all four of the other super centers. Nate rebounds on a par with any of them and is generally reliable on defense. He is thoroughly capable of getting hot on offense with either his long fall-away jumper or his hook shot. He has also established himself as a premier inside man when it comes to obtaining and taking full advantage of mismatches with smaller men. When he was with the Warriors, where he spent the first 10 years of his career, he had the pick-and-roll down to a science, using either a guard or a forward as an accomplice.

It is expected that Walton will be a worthy match for the more experienced stars in time. In fact, his total contribution in a game more closely resembles that of Thurmond than it does any of the others.

The public misconception of what constitutes a good performance from a center was magnified when Milwaukee met Portland in an exhibition game in October of 1974. To the competing teams, it was "us versus them," but to the media and the more than thirteen thousand fans who jammed Dayton Arena to witness the game, it was Abdul-Jabbar versus Walton. When Kareem wound up outscoring the newcomer by a 34–15 margin to spark a Milwaukee triumph, it was widely hailed as a singular victory for him at the expense of Walton. He certainly didn't view it that way, and neither did those who recognized that there will be very few nights when Walton will outscore Abdul-Jabbar. The fact is that Kareem's job on the team is not the same as Bill's. Each job differs because it reflects not only the skills of the men's teammates but their own strengths and skills as well.

Whomever the comparisons concern—Abdul-Jabbar versus Cowens, McAdoo versus Lanier, Paultz versus Gilmore—it must be remembered that each man has a specific role in relation to his team, and that the only real issue is whether the player accomplished what he was supposed to within the team concept. Each match-up is fascinating in its own way, but the outcome of statistical battles is rarely the determining factor in deciding a game.

This much, however, is certain: The center is the most important man on a professional team. As Satch Sanders used to say, every team needs a horse.

This much is certain: The center is the most important man on a professional team. As Satch Sanders used to say, every team needs a horse.

The Power and the Speed
Forwards

he most drastic change in the way the modern game of professional basketball is played, as opposed to the way it was played in the fifties, has taken place at the forward position. That the change is entirely for the better is without question. Basketball has been transformed from a game in which size was beginning to mean everything into one in which relative size is less important than style of play. As a result, many players standing between 6 feet 4 inches and 6 feet 6 inches have been saved from lives of misery at guard.

It had become almost axiomatic in the late fifties, and right on up through the mid-sixties, that guards were people under 6 feet 6 inches and centers were people over 6 feet 10 inches. Anyone under 6 feet 6 inches simply could not be a forward, nor was there much chance of a man under 6 feet 10 inches being tried at center. From thinking thus came such ludicrous experiments as having Nate Thurmond (6-11) play forward and Dave DeBusschere (a not especially speedy 6-6) play guard.

Once upon a time there had been an ideal forward combination—one that, in retrospect, set the tone for the way the game is played today. Back when the Minneapolis Lakers were basketball's best team, the starting forwards were Vern Mikklesen, a rugged 6-foot 7-inch inside man, and Jim Pollard, a smooth 6-foot 5-inch forward who could run and move beautifully. They blended not only with each other but with center George Miken as well. Were they playing today, they would be referred to as the "power forward" (Mikklesen) and the "quick forward" (Pollard),

and they would be hailed as an ideal pairing, which they most certainly were.

The Lakers discovered their forward duo somewhat by accident. "They had no concept of the quick forward or the power forward," explains Red Auerbach, who coached against them at the time. "Pollard and Mikklesen were the two best forwards of any description that they had, so they played them." Auerbach also admits that Pollard and Mikklesen were very much a modern duo. Pollard could shoot from the outside, but what he did best was drive.

For some reason teams did not see fit to emulate the Lakers. Instead, they sought the biggest and strongest forwards they could find and proceeded to put two of them in the lineup. One of the few small forwards of prominence in the fifties was Philadelphia's Paul Arizin, who, at 6 feet 4 inches, possessed a very accurate jump shot and was one of the league's leading scorers. The only other prominent 6-foot 4-inch forward was St. Louis' Cliff Hagan, who was immensely strong, with powerful hands, and who favored an inside game that included a lot of hook shots.

All the top forwards of the era had strong moves to the hoop, but none more so than Dolph Schayes, the magnificent star of the Syracuse Nationals, who played for 15 years. No analysis of great forwards is complete without including him. Schayes was the prototype forward of the forties and fifties. He came from New York (NYU), which meant that he was a smart player He was 6 feet 7 inches tall, and strong. He was always among the league's rebound leaders—once the NBA began keeping that statistic in 1951. The offense Schayes displayed was varied. He had as a primary weapon a two-hand set shot, which he

could launch accurately from 30 feet away. But what he especially loved to do was drive, an act equated with manhood in his mind. In the first half-century of pre-Elgin Baylor basketball, there was never a man who could get the driving three-point play better than Schayes.

Forwards in the NBA have always done their share of scoring. The first great scorer in the history of the league was a 6-foot 5-inch forward named Joe Fulks, the first scoring champion (23.2 in 1946–47), whose single game record of 63 points, set on February 10, 1949, withstood the efforts of all the great scorers to break it until Baylor himself pumped in 64 points against the Celtics on November 8, 1959. The first man to break the 2,000-point barrier in a season was a bald-headed forward for the Detroit Pistons named George Yardley. He scored 2,001 points in 1957–58.

The first great stars in the ABA were forwards, namely Julius Erving, George McGinnis, Dan Issel, Roger Brown, and Willie Wise, not to mention the defecting Spencer Haywood and Billy Cunningham.

Playing forward is the best way to sample all phases of basketball. A well-rounded forward participates in every aspect of the game. He must shoot, pass, rebound, and set picks, whereas a guard may have no rebounding responsibilities and a center no need to pass.

The mere fact of becoming a professional after playing less demanding ball in college makes life difficult for young players, but it seems that far more young cornermen encounter problems than do their center and guard counterparts. The reason: most of them are converted centers. One of the problems with standing anywhere over 6 feet 3 inches in high school is that you have an outstanding chance of being made the center. The problem continues into college if you stand taller than 6 feet 5 inches.

Playing forward is the best way to sample all phases of basketball. A well-rounded forward participates in every aspect of the game. He must shoot, pass, rebound, and set picks.

There is simply no comparison between life spent with one's back to the basket and life spent facing it. The options are so greatly limited and the choices so obviously clear for a center. A forward has a great many more problems. Bars throughout America are populated by people who could have played center in the NBA if they were 2 to 10 inches taller. Many are college stars who couldn't adjust to playing forward.

Rebounding, for one thing, is different for a cornerman than it is for a center. A forward must learn to seize available openings to get where he's going at exactly the right moment. A center, on the other hand, has only to turn and jump. He is already near the basket. And while most centers haven't the slightest idea what the term "blocking out" means, no decent forward rebounder can ignore it. Because a forward could be almost anywhere on the court when a shot goes up, he must make a simple policy decision regarding a possible rebound. He must ask himself, "Should I bother going after the ball?" The results of a wrong decision can be disastrous.

Learning when to go for the ball and when not to is one of the most important lessons a professional coach must teach a young forward. It makes no sense to have all five offensive players converging within a radius of 10 feet for the basket on every shot. Against a fast-breaking team, such as the Celtics or Braves, the end result would be a succession of easy baskets that would break the game open early. On the other hand, there are plenty of opportunities for extra shots if a forward pays attention and recognizes the proper moment to crash the boards. The same is true when the forward is on defense. At times he should be thinking about releasing downcourt to start his own fast break instead of fruitlessly aiding rebounders who may not need help. None of these decisions need bother a center, since he is almost invariably involved in the rebounding action.

Defense is also different for a cornerman than it is for a center. A center is often his team's "court of last resort" underneath to stop an opponent's would-be score. Though a forward does not have that particular responsibility, he can contribute in a variety of ways to his opponent's defensive breakdown. He must move quickly. The average pro forward is a lot quicker than the average college center. The forward must also worry about being picked off, a situation that seldom materializes for a college center. Learning to avoid or to fight off picks is a common problem for young forwards—as well as for guards.

Forwards encounter difficulty on offense as much as they do on defense. Say, for example, that a certain player displayed a good 15-foot jumper as a collegian, but that he almost invariably took the shot when wide open because the rival center was told to stay back or because the opposing team was playing zone defense. That same player attempts to become a pro forward and discovers that he is now being tightly guarded, that his pet shot isn't as accurate when there is a hand in his face and a hand on his hip. Exit prospect.

There is almost no way to become an outstanding forward without acquiring a sound mental approach to the game. Forwards, if not careful, are susceptible to the back-door play. They must not give up the baseline to clever drivers and at the same time they must learn to go to the proper open spot on offense.

The modern approach to forward deployment was fostered by Red Auerbach, who shocked the basketball world by making a forward out of Frank Ramsey, the 6-foot 3-inch All-American from Kentucky. It should first be pointed out that Ramsey was also a guard at Boston, and was, in fact, the first of two great Boston "sixth" men, the forward-

guard monster who would come in and give the team a needed lift at either position.

Auerbach's use of Ramsey came about because of the extraordinary talents of Bill Russell. Auerbach had an uncanny ability to piece together a jigsaw puzzle of complementary men with mismatched talents, a tradition that exists on today's Celtics.

"My theory about the sixth man," Auerbach says, "is that when I make that first, or even that second, substitution, I should be improving the team, and not be decreasing the production. I felt that with a guy like Russell, who was a great, great rebounder, all I would need from the quick forward would be someone smart enough to box out.

"I knew there were two ends of the court, and that if I had Ramsey in there some big guy would

Learning when to go for the ball
and when not to is one of the most
important lessons a professional
coach must teach a forward.

125

have to wind up guarding him. The best evidence of this came when San Francisco had Chamberlain [7–1], Thurmond [6–11], and Tom Meschery [6–6] in the same front line. I put Heinsohn [6–7] on Meschery and Ramsey on Thurmond. There was no way in the world that Thurmond could stay with Ramsey. Russell and Heinsohn, mostly Russell, still got the ball and we had no trouble.''

Thus was born the quick forward. The amazing thing, however, is that few teams followed the Boston lead, even though the concept was working well for the Celtics.

The trend to automatically convert 6-foot 5-inch college forwards into guards may have reached its most ridiculous proportions when the Knicks tried to make, within the space of two years, guards out of Cazzie Russell and Bill Bradley. Both were All-Americans of the most heralded variety, and both had the capacity to give rivals a lot of trouble. But each man spent nightmarish games trying to play a position for which he was totally unsuited. It is difficult now, watching Bradley hound John Havlicek all over the court, to conceive of him as being a guard. If Havlicek could play forward, why not Bradley? One of the few people who recognized the corner as Bradley's proper home was Auerbach. He, almost alone, understood the value of the quick forward in the right situation. But the Knicks at the time had both Walt Bellamy and Willis Reed in their starting frontline and they didn't need another rebounding forward.

Bradley's value as a forward lies in what he can contribute to the overall flow of the offense, as well as in his comprehension of New York's defensive aim. When people think of the offensive Bradley, they think of his soft jump shots from the perimeter, but his value far transcends that. He is a superb passer, and his ability to think two or three steps ahead enables the Knicks to do things

McGinnis, who is often mentioned in the same breath as Erving by ABA enthusiasts, "is overpowering."

126

on the floor that are denied to other teams. It has been said that it is a pity Bradley turned pro, that to have seen him as a collegian was to see basketball played by its near-perfect practitioner. His movement and thinking against a zone defense or against the gang-up (box and one, for example) defenses of Princeton's frustrated rivals were marvelous to behold. His collegiate star was so bright, his image so untarnished, that many felt he could only do himself harm by turning professional.

Though he has not proven to be a superstar (whatever that means), he has fulfilled his promise as a superior team player, which is all that can be asked of him. The Bradley–DeBusschere corner duo the Knicks were able to employ for five and a half seasons went unsurpassed as a cohesive, thinking forward pair. The quick forward concept pioneered by Auerbach must not be construed to mean "small and big." The quick forward can be as big as 6 feet 9 inches and the power forward can be as small as 6 feet 4 inches. It all depends on how they play.

Bob Love (6-8), can be called Chicago's "quick" forward and Don Adams (6-7) can be labeled his club's "power" forward. The former is a finesse player who sneaks around behind a maze of picks for economical 6- to 15-foot jumpers while standing on tiptoes. He is quick, deceptive, and he has a fast release on his shot, which he propels with an almost imperceptible flick of the wrist. Conversely, Adams is an aggressive ox of a man who plays a physical, but cerebral game. He is called upon to defend all types of players. His normal defensive assignment against Boston is to guard John Havlicek, who can hardly be classified as slow. Adams challenges Havlicek by trying to slow him down, a feat he accomplishes by any means at his disposal. And thus he answers to the nickname, "Smart."

There are many other size incongruities in the

pros. Connie Hawkins (6-8), for example, is hardly a powerful man, while Bill Bridges (6-6) is able to dismantle tractor trailers with his bare hands. Again, playing style is what counts.

A great power forward can make up for the lack of a truly dominating center, a fact to which both the Knicks and Celtics can attest. When Willis Reed began to lose his effectiveness, his injuries robbing his powerful body of its full strength, the Knicks continued to survive, and even to win an amazing championship in 1973, because in Dave DeBusschere they had the consummate power forward. In order to be successful, a team must have a solid inside presence, and if it can't come completely from the center spot, then it can come from a power forward.

DeBusschere, who never won his share of postseason awards despite the immense lip service paid his talents by the media, may have been the best combination of talents to play forward in his time. At 6 feet 6 inches and 225 pounds, he was more than competitive in terms of muscle. He had played center enough in high school and college to know his way around the pivot. He was agile enough to have been considered a prospective guard in the old days. His offense was tremendously varied—he could connect on a 25-foot jumper, drive to the basket, or muscle through heavy traffic for a tap-in. Though he clearly earned the tag ''power forward'' by his physical presence, he could also handle the quick cornermen. For several years, New York's humiliating domination of the Bucks was due in large measure to DeBusschere's ability to consistently shackle the exceedingly quick Bob Dandrige. Even the fabled Doctor J. (Julius Erving) found that DeBusschere could contend with him when their teams met during the exhibition circuit.

Probably the most graphic demonstration of the value of a power forward in recent times began

The ideal forward combination is power and speed. The former makes up for the lack of a dominating center, the latter is hard to stop.

Big men get the ball off the boards and, in many cases, put it back into the basket. But ask the average fan who he pays his money to see play and more than likely he'll tell you the little guys, the guards.

The reason is simple. The guards are the ones with whom the fan can identify. Bob Cousy's overwhelming popularity was because he, at 6 feet 1 inch, was closer to the average guy in size than most of the other players. Though 6 feet 1 inch is still at least 2 inches over the national average, it is not a towering height, whereas 6 feet 6 inches is. Fans feel out of touch with players that tall. When people saw Cousy out-foxing tall men in a game commonly believed to be the exclusive province of monsters, they derived a vicarious thrill that far exceeded any other pleasure they got from viewing the game.

This excitement remains today, generated by Nate Archibald, Calvin Murphy, Mack Calvin, Dean Meminger, Ernie DiGregorio, Kevin Porter, Don ("Slick") Watts, and other men under, or near, 6 feet tall who are playing professional basketball successfully. Their exploits are appreciated far more than those of the bigger men who excel at the game, and the reason hasn't changed. Fans are able to identify with them.

There is a certain amount of irony to all this, inasmuch as the amazing ability possessed by the small men of today is as far removed from the scope of the average fan as is the skill possessed by the big men. Big men bring to the game height and fantastic agility, but the small men bring to it agility, quickness, and guile.

Because there are a few men who have been able to compete with the Brobdingnagians, the fan feels that, if circumstances were right, perhaps he could too, forgetting that for every extremely small man playing pro basketball, there are thousands of others who would like to, but who aren't. In many cases, the addition of another inch or two would have made that player a pro. The selection process is exact and rigid.

To succeed, small guards must have great determination. "All my career," explains DiGregorio, who is the first player in a dozen years whose style can adequately be compared to Cousy's, "people have said I was too slow, too small, or too fat. It's been one thing after another. But I've always managed to overcome it."

There was a time, however, when he almost certainly would have been denied the opportunity to compete. Remember the aforementioned span in pro basketball history when every man coming out of college in the 6-foot 5- or 6-inch range was tried as a guard? Well, who do you suppose the victims of that policy were? The small guards.

During the sixties, the two smallest men in the NBA were John Egan and Larry Costello. Egan was always listed as 5 feet 11 inches tall, primarily so his teams could refer to him as "the only man under six feet in the NBA." Costello was about an inch taller. The men had two things in common: each was exceptionally fast and each was smart. Both men wound up as coaches in the league, testimony in itself to their thinking ability.

K. C. Jones wasn't much bigger than either of them, but he had the good fortune to play for the "right" team, the Celtics. It is possible that had he shown up at any other training camp,

The amazing ability
possessed
by the small men
of today is as far
removed from
the scope of the
average fan as is
the skill possessed
by the big men.

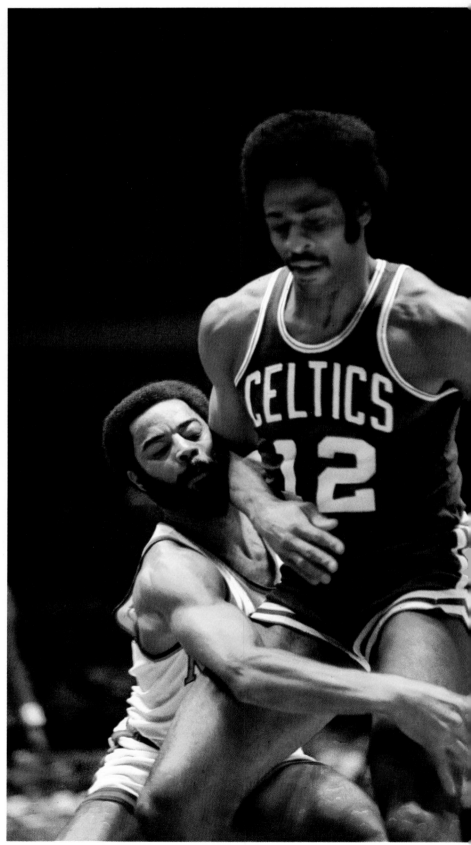

Even Cousy supported Archibald's claim that he was ignored by coaches who had passed him up in the draft and who didn't want to be reminded of their error by his embarrassing presence in the All-Star Game.

Nate reacted by ripping off a scoring streak as the second half of the season unfolded, finishing with a 28.2-points-a-game average, shooting an excellent 48 percent from the floor. He was serving notice that he was a man to be reckoned with. The next season he put on the most dominating performance in one season that any little man could ever have dreamed of.

So dominant was Archibald that Cousy all but turned over the entire team to him, making the tiny guard the center of the offense. Archibald was so effective in attracting attention on the court that backcourt teammate Matt Guokas wound up with a slew of unmolested corner jumpers to connect on 59 percent of his shots.

The season after Archibald's dramatic breakthrough into basketball's most honored circle was an extremely frustrating one. On the opening night of the 1973–74 campaign, he was stepped on by Chicago's massive center, Tom Boerwinkle, who is 7 feet tall and weighs 275 pounds. For Archibald, who answers to the name of "Tiny," there couldn't have been a bigger mismatch. The injury to his Achilles tendon kept him out of the lineup for 47 games and rendered him ineffective in most of the games he did play. However, he had time to recuperate in the ensuing off-season, and by the start of the 1974–75 season he was ready to resume his quicksilver ways.

Exciting guards have fascinated the public since basketball's inception. When the game was played with the center jump (pre-1938), there was a premium on ball handling and ball control because it wasn't easy to get the ball back once a team lost it. Guards controlled the play effectively.

Undoubtedly the greatest influence on guard play in the history of the game has been Bob Cousy, who came out of New York City to enter Holy Cross after World War II and who left such a collegiate legacy that there are thousands of New Englanders who haven't ventured near a college gymnasium since his departure. They believe the game isn't worth watching without him.

Cousy's contribution to modern offense is incalculable. He pioneered the sleight of hand—which is seen so much today—with his instinctive behind-the-back dribbles and passes. He spawned a generation of imitators, almost none of whom possessed his marvelous physical gifts. For a man 6 feet 1 inch tall, he had exceptionally long arms and big hands.

Cousy refined the art of playmaking to such an extent that he hasn't been seriously challenged by his immediate successors. Many guards who are labeled as "playmakers" are not playmakers at all. They are reactionaries who can spot and hit open men, which in itself is an admirable trait. But the difference between them and Cousy is that Cousy created the open men—treating the floor as a chessboard—by manipulation and well-conceived actions. It is not a science that can be taught easily and, in fact, may not be a science at all. Only Lenny Wilkens, Walt Frazier, Oscar Robertson, John Havlicek (yes, Havlicek, close to being the best guard today), and Ernie DiGregorio can lay claim to being true playmakers in the NBA. In the ABA, perhaps the best pure playmaker in the league's history has been Bill Melchionni, although there is a little-known, elfin-looking guard, James Joseph O'Brien, who knows how to make a play. Jimmy O'Brien played his college ball for Bob Cousy at Boston College.

Cousy was the most spectacular and innovative guard of his or any other time, but even in his day he had some serious rivals. Among them

Few rosters of the sixties contained small guards. Fortunately for the paying customer, that feeling no longer exists in professional ball.

were Bobby Davis, (''Tricky'') Dick McGuire, and Slater Martin. Many people believe that McGuire was actually Cousy's equal—perhaps even his superior—at the technical art of passing. He didn't throw as many passes away, but neither did he attempt as many daring maneuvers. Cousy is generally acknowledged unequaled when it comes to creativity.

The ideal modern pairing contains a play-maker and a shooter. College people refer to the former as a ''number one guard'' and the latter as a ''number two guard.'' Although the pros don't always employ that terminology, the intent is the same. Any team that can blend a number one and a number two is in good shape.

Nothing, of course, could be more ideal than a guard who is a legitimate combination of a number one and a number two. Men such as Robertson, Jerry West, and Frazier can be described this way, as can Havlicek—when he's playing in the backcourt.

It was fitting that Robertson and West, whose careers paralleled so closely, should retire in concert prior to the 1974–75 season. Most knowledgeable observers rank them as the two best guards who ever played the game, although there are those who hold out for Cousy, despite his comparative personal scoring deficiency.

Oscar was a technically perfect backcourt performer in all phases of the game except one: there were many men who were better at running the fast break. But Oscar had no equal in his time directing a half court offense.

Remember Frank Powers' assessment? ''If I were going to find a model for a young guard, it would have to be Oscar. I would tell the boy to dribble like Oscar, pass like Oscar, and shoot like Oscar.''

Economy of motion was Robertson's trademark. He was basketball's answer to Hank Aaron.

When Chenier came into the league in 1972 as a hardship case out of the University of California, people blinked their eyes in disbelief.

146

It was simply not in Oscar's nature to be flamboyant—except when it came to disagreeing with referees. He performed for 14 seasons, but apparently in his heart he believed he had never committed a personal foul.

Just as Cousy was responsible for countless imitators among the white youth of America, so did Robertson become the idol of millions of young blacks. Several of his disciples in style are present in the NBA, most notably Frazier and Phil Chenier.

There is no question about Frazier's debt to Oscar. Despite the ostentatiousness of his personal life, Frazier plays the game with a minimum of fuss. He only does what he has to do on the floor, and he never goes out of his way to show off. Unlike more exuberant types like Randy Smith or Fred Carter, Frazier doesn't dunk the ball on every occasion, although he could easily do so. He is more dedicated to defense than Oscar was for most of his career, and as a result comes up with crowd-pleasing steals, for which some people would call him flamboyant. But even in those moments Frazier is more subtle than flashy.

One self-styled descendant of Robertson's is Boston's Jo Jo White, a remarkably dead-pan guard from the University of Kansas. White pays some tribute to Frazier, who is a year and a half older than he is, saying how much he admires his on-court demeanor (if Frazier complains once a year to officials, it's big news in Madison Square Garden). But it really is Oscar whom White is emulating. He, too, is an avowed non-dunker, even though he can get high off the floor. "Sure, I could do it," he explains. "But there's always a chance I could miss, and I'd rather have the easy two points."

When Chenier came into the league in 1972 as a hardship case out of the University of California, people blinked their eyes in disbelief. "It's

148

The ideal modern pairing contains a
playmaker and a shooter. Any team that
can blend the two is in good shape.

another Frazier!'' they exclaimed. Indeed, the physical resemblance, as well as the controlled, unruffled playing style, was so reminiscent of the vaunted Clyde that it was unnerving. In the ensuing years, Chenier has proved that the comparisons of their playing style were not entirely unwarranted. His scoring production rose in his first three years from 12.3 to 19.7 to 21.9 points per game, and his steadiness on defense improved accordingly. In the 1973–74 season, he and West were the only two players in the league with more steals than personal fouls, and he had played many more minutes than the Los Angeles great.

Chenier also found himself compared to the master. "Remember," inquired teammate Mike Riordan, "how Oscar wouldn't take an eleven-footer if he could get a ten-footer, or a ten-footer if he could get a nine-footer? Well, Phil is starting to get some of those Oscar instincts into his game."

The reason the Robertson style is so worth emulating for a big guard (Frazier, White, and Chenier are all at least 6 feet 3 inches tall; Oscar himself was 6 feet 5 inches) is that it works. None of them possesses the flat-out speed of the smaller dynamos. It behooves them, therefore, to use their size to maneuver for the best possible shot—the way Oscar did. With the increasing number of small guards in the league these days, the taller ones can often get their pick of medium-range turnaround jumpers by exercising a little patience.

As great as Oscar was, there are an equal number of backers who boost his contemporary, West, as the best guard in history, though statistically there is a remarkable parity between the two. Robertson retired as the second leading scorer of all time; West bowed out as the third, but finished with a better per-game average. Even so, they were not really the same type of player.

West was the greatest shooting, or number

Others are simply solid citizens who do a little bit of everything well, but who possess a strong competitive spirit that enables them to out-perform their more gifted rivals.

150

two, guard in either league. He could operate efficiently with the ball, but his real skill was operating without it, emerging at the right moment to take advantage of a well-timed pass and a pick, behind which he launched his soft jump shot or began a twisting drive. Robertson always had the ball. Nobody will ever know if he could have done anything without it—he never tried.

West was a dogged defender. Along with John Havlicek, he epitomized the concept of the hard-nosed, two-way athlete more than any other player in history. Every basket scored against him during his long career was earned. In Oscar's later days he displayed defensive prowess, but there were long stretches earlier in his career when he paid scant attention to defense.

One thing is certain: From the time Cousy retired following the 1962–63 season until the dawn of the seventies, Oscar Robertson and Jerry

West dominated postseason backcourt honors. They were the NBA All-Star guard pair from 1961–62 through 1966–67. It must have been frustrating for Philadelphia's Hal Greer, five times runner-up to the leaders in that span (and seven times a second team All-Star, a number exceeded only by Bill Russell, who finished on the second squad eight times), and for Sam Jones of Boston, who made the second team three times.

Greer is often hailed as the consummate middle distance shooter, a title he nailed down for good with a dazzling 8-for-8 shooting show in the 1968 All-Star Game, the last one ever held in the old Madison Square Garden. The entire nation saw his virtuoso shooting skills on display that night. He carted off the Most Valuable Player award on one of the highlight evenings of his distinguished career.

Jones was the successor to another Boston

Guard defense is perhaps the roughest of all. Certainly mistakes are magnified more, and there is considerable chance for embarrassment.

great, Bill Sharman. Sam was a pure shooter and, more specifically, a pure bank shooter. He and latter-day marvel Rudy Tomjanovich may very well be the two greatest exponents of that fascinating art. He is often cited as the best clutch shooter in Celtic history, and the strange part is that his contemporaries assure anyone who will listen that Sam took every one of those big shots under duress. Greatness was thrust on him; and he had to be forced to accept it.

Great shooting guards have always been a part of modern basketball history. Whether the discussion is of the two-hand set shooting habits of Carl Braun (who favored the two-hand overhead method) or Larry Costello; the medium range accuracy of Sharman, generally believed to be the premier shooter of the fifties; the wizardry of West, who went unsurpassed in the sixties; or any of today's stars, the pattern remains clear. Most guards are shooters.

Certainly at no time in basketball history has shooting from the backcourt, or from long distances, no matter who is shooting, been any better than it is today. Attempting to select the best shooter or shooters is an impossible task. Virtually every team in pro basketball has at least one potentially devastating outside shooter who must be checked closely.

Consider the following names: Frazier, White, Chenier, Gail Goodrich, Pete Maravich, Charley Scott, the Brothers Van Arsdale (Tom and Dick), Earl Monroe, Austin Carr, Fred Brown, Nate Archibald, Calvin Murphy, Ernie DiGregorio, Geoff Petrie, Jeff Mullins, Dick Snyder, Jon McGlocklin, Jim Price, Mike Newlin, Louie Dampier, Jimmy Jones, Ralph Simpson, Bo Lamar, Rick Mount. And those are just the guards. These men, plus many others, can hurt teams from the outside, even from as far away as 25 feet.

Guards have a value that far transcends shoot-

Certainly at no time in basketball history has shooting from the backcourt—no matter who is shooting—been any better than it is today.

154

ing. In fact, some of the best guards are not premier shooters. Some are more defensively oriented; others are essentially playmakers. Still others are simply solid citizens who do a little bit of everything well, but who possess a strong competitive spirit that enables them to out-perform their more gifted rivals.

Such a duo has belonged for some time to the Chicago Bulls, whose backcourt pairing of Jerry Sloan and Norm Van Lier is one of the finest in league history.

Van Lier has obvious physical attributes, including speed, quickness, and playmaking ability. He has one league-assists crown to his credit (when he played for Cousy at Cincinnati) and would almost undoubtedly have won another one or two if he had played in a different type of offense than the one employed by coach Dick Motta of the Bulls. He is not, however, a destructive shooter, although he does enjoy his hot moments. He is a good shooter with the game on the line and that makes him a dangerous man.

All Sloan has to offer his coach, teammates, and fans is "blood, toil, tears, and sweat." Nothing has ever come, nor will it ever come, easy to this rugged competitor from the oil fields of southern Illinois. He has no obvious physical attributes except for a raw-boned body that is, at first-glance, too big for a guard and too small for a forward.

What makes the pair so special? Their defensive instincts. Van Lier is 6 feet 1 inch tall and exceedingly quick. There is hardly a man who can get by him when he chooses to play aggressive defense. He is afraid of no one and does not hesitate to step in front of the biggest players in order to draw a charging foul and obtain the precious basketball for his team's deliberate offense.

Sloan, between 6 feet 5 and 6 inches tall, can hardly be classified as "quick." But he makes up for his overall lack of speed with a determina-tion and dedication to defense that will not allow him to quit on anyone. He uses arms, knees, legs, hands, and if need be, chin, forehead, and nose in order to slow down his foes. If an official objects to his tactics and signifies his disapproval by calling a foul, Sloan is likely to stomp after him with the basketball wrapped in his meaty paw, a wild-eyed look on his face, and heatedly challenge the referee's manhood, intelligence, and moral character.

Opponents respect and, in some cases, hate him. Some fervently believe he has deliberately hurt people. Others go out of their way to hurt him —he has probably been banged up more than any other guard playing the game today. His coach would love to employ him as a third forward more often (there is no doubt that he can do the job off the boards) but hesitates to do so before the playoffs for fear he will thoroughly exhaust himself banging away at the monsters who lurk underneath the backboards in the NBA. Sloan gets physically involved enough just playing in the backcourt against more normal-sized opponents.

The only statistical category in which Sloan rates high on an annual basis is rebounds. In fact, both he and Van Lier (despite his size) are among the league's premier rebounding backcourtmen. The team couldn't function without that important contribution, because Chet Walker and Bob Love are never among the top rebounding forwards in the league. The guards simply do what they must do to win and, in this case, rebounding is one of those things.

Sloan and Van Lier have not always received the credit for their team's success that Walker and Love have. The forwards are both high scorers, and a significant percentage of the Chicago offense has always been directed at them. Those in the know, however, have acknowledged the contributions of both guards.

Few players have ever combined the passing, playmaking, and shooting abilities that Pete Maravich possesses.

Many guards come into the league after life-long careers as forwards, just as many forwards come into pro ball following long apprenticeships as centers. The transition is not easy.

Two problems are ball handling and defense. The ability to handle the ball is relative. What is considered to be quality ball handling at center is somewhat less than is required in the corner. The same goes for forward ball handling as compared to guard ball handling. There are so many more defensive guards with exceptionally quick hands and body movement than there are big men, that a person unsure of his ball handling is prone to panic and is likely to fall apart completely on the floor. Guards need poise, and this is one of the traits professional scouts look for in a young backcourtman. The pro guard who cannot handle a decent press is in for a lot of trouble.

What makes ball handling skills so crucial is the 24-second clock. A classic example of the clock's role occurred in the 1974 NBA finals between Boston and Milwaukee. In order to harass the Bucks and keep the ball from getting in to Kareem Abdul-Jabbar, where he could do something with it, the Celtics embarked on a full court press, primarily to force the Bucks to use as many of those valuable 24 seconds as possible when they set up a play. A secondary aim was to cause direct turnovers. The strategy worked perfectly in the first game. Boston achieved both goals by constantly leaving the Bucks with fewer than 10 seconds to run off a decent set play—when they weren't having the ball stolen or throwing it away. Milwaukee guard Ron ("Fritz") Williams, a seasoned professional, was so exposed by the Boston tactics he was benched for the remainder of the seven-game series.

There is almost no way a team can hope to win a championship without at least one guard who is an excellent ball handler and has the poise to direct an offense. If a would-be contender has as its backcourt two excellent shooters, but neither of them is a decent ball handler, then it is practically doomed to quick regular-season extinction.

Defense is another common failing of young guards. From the simple standpoint of geography, guard defense is perhaps the roughest of all. Certainly, mistakes are magnified more, and there is considerable chance for embarrassment.

Consider the guard's defensive floor position, which is generally somewhere between the foul circle and the mid-court line. He must watch the actions of the man he is guarding—which is enough of a concern—whether the rival be a small, quick penetrator or a bigger, slower shooter. But more important, he must develop an awareness of the entire court. Picks could be coming at him from either side, or from behind, and a guard must learn how to cope with them. The first thing he must learn is to heed the counsel of his teammates who, hopefully, are yelling warnings such as "Pick left!" or "Watch out on your right!" In such cases, he will more or less survive or perish in concert with his mates. The pro team that doesn't engage in lively conversation on defense will almost certainly wind up the loser.

The defensive guard must learn to slide through, or physically fight through picks. Picks (or screens) can be disastrous, even if a proper switch is made. Because few offenses involve one guard setting a pick for another guard, if a guard gets himself involved in a switch it almost invariably means he is now defending a bigger man. If he is in too deep to the basket, there is almost nothing he can do except gamble. Perhaps he can step in front of the offensive man ("front him," as the players say) and risk a lob pass thrown to

There is almost no way a team can hope to win a championship without at least one guard who is an excellent ball handler, with poise to direct an offense.

6

A Will to Win
Coaches
and Strategy

One has a doctorate in education and executes pirouettes from a kneeling position, something Nureyev himself may never have attempted. Another collects old fight films, likes slim little cigars, and won't hesitate to take one of his recalcitrant stars into the back alley for a showdown.

There is one who uses words like "inculcate," who is an accomplished life insurance salesman and amateur painter, and who is working on the great NBA novel.

You may recall still another from his very famous television commercial for that equally famous public utility.

NBA coaches all, they have chosen to involve themselves in a profession that should carry ulcer insurance as a clause in every contract. Who, after all, needs the aggravation? Who should have to put up with endless travel, boring practices, spoiled athletes, nerve-racking games, adverse officiating decisions, practically nonexistent security, and in many cases, the lack of recognition that goes along with the job? The answer, of course, is men like the aforementioned, men who are driven and motivated by the need to be a leader. Some coaches, like Utah's ex-mentor Jack Gardner, who kept a bottle of milk handy for his ulcer, find they can neither live with it—nor without it. The Napoleon in them cannot be suppressed.

How important is a professional coach? This question is asked by followers of any pro sport, as they watch coaches hired and fired with regularity. Does coaching make any difference, or is a team's talent the sole criterion? Can a bad team win with a great coach? Conversely, can a bad coach prevent a great team from winning? Though these questions cannot be answered with surety, there is enough evidence on hand to form certain convictions.

Baseball offers the classic example of a rags-to-riches mentor in Casey Stengel. He was regarded as little more than a harmless, beguiling fool when he managed the Brooklyn Dodgers and Boston Braves in the National League. When the New York Yankees rescued him from semi-oblivion in the Pacific Coast League to make him their manager in 1949, baseball experts could hardly believe it. Why would the Yankees entrust their ball club to a stand-up comedian who had never before enjoyed success managing in the majors?

Stengel fooled them. He won five world championships in his first five years. People then decided that, since this was the same man who had managed the losing Dodgers and Braves, the teams must have done it all, that he was not responsible for their losses. It was only in retrospect that people appreciated the job he had actually done. By his insistence on platooning certain of his ball players, he had coaxed the maximum from his team. Some of the platooned players complained bitterly at the time about their part-time status, but they all later admitted that Stengel's deployment of them had improved their production and, in some cases, prolonged their careers.

Stengel had been neither a bum while he managed the previous teams nor a genius when he handled the Yankees. In fact, until he became successful with the Yankees, eventually bowing out with 10 pennants in 12 years, no one bothered to suggest that perhaps he had gotten the most out of the two previous teams.

And that is what coaching,

practice session. A good scout sits close to the action to pick up the verbal signals. By watching a team just once, he can diagram a dozen or more plays, including tap-off plays and out-of-bounds plays. In many cases, he is only looking for new developments, because if both he and the coach whose team he is scouting have been around for a while, there probably isn't a great deal that isn't already known. The scout is happiest when he is responsible for following only one of the two teams playing. Between charting a team's offense and watching for its defensive tendencies, he has his hands full. It is almost humanly impossible to scout two teams at once.

In addition to scouting reports, films are coming more and more into vogue as training aids. Some teams have been using videotapes for several years. It is common practice for the film of the last game the Knicks played against a certain opponent to be shown while the team is dressing at home for another game with that team.

New York Nets' coach Kevin Loughery is one of the more forceful exponents of videotape. Disgusted at his team's abominable performance in the rebound department during the first half of a game early in the 1974–75 season, he ordered the tape delivered to the locker room. Instead of talking, he showed the team exactly how inept they'd been, after which they rallied to win the game that day.

Scouting and postgame analyzing reached a zenith in the basketball world in the 1974 Boston–Milwaukee playoff finals. This series has often been referred to as the "Coaches Series" because, almost as much as Kareem Abdul-Jabbar, John Havlicek, and Dave Cowens, the coaches created the excitement.

The teams alternated victories throughout the seven-game series, which was the lowest-scoring but hardly the worst-played series of the post-24-second-clock era. Heinsohn and Killilea gained the upper hand in the running battle of one-upmanship with Larry Costello and Hubie Brown of Milwaukee with a sensational Boston victory in the opening game. From then on, the series became a chess match, with the Bucks' duo managing to come up with the answer to every Boston tactic once they had a chance to witness the strategy.

Costello and Brown certainly thought they had the Celtics well scouted, having played them four times in the regular season as well as in several games in preceding seasons. They were not, however, prepared for a new Boston offense, which sent men down the middle when Milwaukee was expecting them to go down the sidelines, and vice versa. In addition, the Celtics worked some beautiful baseline exchanges, with the forwards picking nicely for each other.

"It was a strong side, weak side, inside and outside offense," smiled Cowens.

"I can't tell you anything," sighed Costello, "until I see the films." It was the classic football coach's lament, but it was the first time the words had ever been uttered after a basketball game.

The battle of wits continued as Milwaukee won the second game. And so it continued until the fateful seventh game. Here the Celtics threw not an offensive, but a defensive wrinkle at the Bucks by leaving forwards Curtis Perry and Cornell Warner open and double- or triple-teaming Abdul-Jabbar, a tactic the Celtics had long eschewed. Thus did the Celtic coaching staff have the last word—because of course there was no game eight.

Pregame preparation for a professional coach rarely involves a Rockne-style pep talk. The pros supply their own motivation, and if they are not stimulated by the time the coach begins his pre-

Disgusted at his team's abominable performance in the rebound department during the first half of a game, he ordered the tape delivered to the locker room.

175

game talk, they never will be. They aren't playing for old alma mater. Instead, a coach usually writes some of the opponents' favorite plays on a blackboard and runs through them, reminding his team about the tendencies of the individual players as he does so. He may also write down a few succinct reminders, such as "Block Out," "Run," or "Good Shots."

The difference between the new and old schools of coaching was evidenced in Boston one night in 1974. Heinsohn was sick with the flu, so Auerbach decided to take over. Assistant coach Killilea put all the Portland plays on the board and ran over them quickly. Then it was Auerbach's turn to speak.

"Hey," he began, "that was very nice. Maybe you'll even retain one or two things from all that. But do you wanna win this game? Block out on the boards and play defense. Now get outta here!"

Coaching can be broken down into three distinct parts—preparation, game coaching, and player relations. Rare is the man who can master all three.

Preparation in terms of pregame scouting has already been explained. But preparation also includes the organization of training camp and the daily practices during the season. A poorly planned training season might result in a loss of early games that could lower the team's standing at the end of the season.

How a coach employs his personnel during exhibition games also affects his team's eventual state of readiness. He must allow a proper amount of playing time for each veteran; players simply cannot get in decent shape by merely practicing and scrimmaging. He must also plan on sufficient playing time for his newcomers, because injuries are not a sometimes thing in modern basketball; they are, regrettably, a way of life. No team goes far these days without having an adequate bench.

Game coaching is the second facet of coaching. A clever coach can pull out a few games for his team during the course of a season, and he can exert great influence in the playoffs, where mistakes are magnified, but unfortunately, coaching an NBA team during a game is not the easiest thing to do.

Ironically, the easiest teams to coach are teams that leave the coach the fewest options, such as the Buffalo Braves of 1973–74. Jack Ramsay had few in-game decisions to make. His team was constructed so as to make his substitution patterns easy. Once the team's general manager Eddie Donovan had strengthened the club by acquiring forward Jack Marin and guard Matt Guokas from Houston for center Kevin Kunnert and guard Dave Wohl, coach Ramsay had a well-defined team. For starting forwards, he had Jim McMillian and Gar Heard. Bob McAdoo was his center. Ernie DiGregorio and Randy Smith were his guards. Marin was the third forward, Guokas the third guard. He had, however, no back-up center. Behind McAdoo there was only journeyman Paul Ruffner, who simply could not be used in meaningful situations.

Ramsay's coaching decisions were clear-cut. He would insert Marin to give either of the forwards a rest and substitute Guokas for one of the guards. On rare occasions he used rookie guard Ken Charles for defensive purposes. When he had to take McAdoo out of a ball game, he generally moved Heard (who, although he is only 6 feet 6 inches tall, is a good jumper) from his power forward spot to center.

As far as substitutions were concerned, Ramsay led a charmed life, unlike his colleagues who had deeper teams and who spent hours second-guessing themselves over the use of this or that player. Ramsay rarely had the chance to second-

The Celtics are perhaps the only team in the league that has tried to draft players solely on their ability to fit conveniently into its style of play.

guess himself, although there were probably times he wished that he could.

Proper substitution is one aspect of game coaching. Another is effective use of time outs. More games have been lost by the injudicious use of the time out than perhaps by any other coaching error.

In the NBA, teams are limited to seven time outs during a game. The important adjunct to that limit is what happens in the fourth quarter, when each team is limited to four time outs. Further, teams are restricted to three time outs during the last two minutes of play. Teams may call additional time outs once they have exhausted the limit, but do so at the expense of a technical foul.

Having time outs to use when a team needs them is of incalculable value in the NBA because the pros have found it quite possible to execute a successful play from midcourt with as little as one second remaining in the game. The rules have been weighted to give teams the maximum opportunity to catch up in a game. The clock is stopped every time the ball goes through the hoop in the last two minutes, a ruling that has saved countless teams from defeat. Consider the following example:

The Portland Trail Blazers were losing to the Houston Rockets by a 108–107 score with three seconds left, when Houston's Rudy Tomjanovich was fouled. He made two free throws. Portland called time out immediately thereafter.

NBA rules call for the subsequent throw-in to be made from midcourt. When play was resumed, Larry Steele passed the ball in to Sidney Wicks, who was allowed to drive through unmolested and stuff the ball. There was one second remaining, but the clock was stopped until Houston put the ball in play.

Houston, however, had no time outs left and found itself facing a Trail Blazer press. Mike New-lin of the Rockets attempted, but was unable to pass the ball in before five seconds of the referees' count had elapsed, and the ball was given back to Portland, which, having one time out left, called it immediately.

The Blazers set up their play. Steele again threw it in, this time to Geoff Petrie, who had come from the far side to cut off a double pick. He took the ball, fired, and hit as the buzzer went off. Portland won, 111–110.

What won the game for Portland? The time outs. Houston had squandered theirs early in the period; the Blazers saved theirs for when needed. Coaching can make a difference.

The proper use of time outs is not, however, restricted to the final seconds of play. There are coaches who simply hate to see things get

The pros supply their own motivation, and if they are not stimulated by the time the coach begins his pregame talk, they never will be.

started on the floor. Suppose, for example, that the Buffalo team hits its first five shots against Detroit and grabs a 10–0 lead in the first minute and a half. If Detroit's coach, Ray Scott, hasn't called a time out by then, it must be that he is asleep. Red Holzman would have called one perhaps no later than 6–0, simply to break, or attempt to break, the Buffalo momentum.

Holzman is probably the best coach at utilizing his time outs in the early and middle parts of a game. Time outs can often serve as brakes, and he seems to have the uncanny knack of calling one at exactly the right moment. Conversely, a team should never think of calling a time out during a hot streak.

A coach's attitude toward the referees is also important. It can often enhance or ruin his team's

179

Substitutions are an important part of
strategy, but sometimes a certain
player should probably never be rested.

chances of winning a game. Officials are human and they are bound to be affected at least subconsciously by the nature of their relationship with a coach on a given night. There isn't a professional coach who can sit through a game without saying something to the officials about the calls, or non-calls, they make. And that's true of high school and college as well. It's simply the nature of the beast. Referees expect comments. They realize the coaches are protecting their livelihoods, that they would be somewhat remiss if they didn't get involved. But just as officials must learn to cope with the idiosyncrasies of professional coaches, so must coaches learn the best way to deal with individual referees.

Coaches generally can be grouped under two headings, screamers and snipers. Screamers, such as Heinsohn, are easily visible to the fans. The snipers (the father-son pair of Dick Motta and Phil Johnson serves as a model), who are liable to be equally despised on their bad nights by officials, never seem to arouse the fans, who can't imagine why they have incurred the officials' anger.

When a Heinsohn leaps up, curls his face into his inimitable sneer, waves his arms, and screams at an official at the top of his lungs, everyone in the arena knows he is inviting the ultimate officiating weapon, the technical foul. When Ramsay, who begins most games from a kneeling position, stomps all the way to midcourt—pulling out a few of his remaining hairs as he goes—and spins around wildly before returning to the sidelines, there is no doubt in anyone's mind that he is upset. Butch van Breda Kolff, who is at least mildly electrifying, has been known to kick over benches and buckets. He holds the unofficial professional record of 38 technicals in one season, a mark he set in the 1973–74 season while coaching the Memphis Tams.

Flamboyancy on the sidelines is not limited to the pros. More than one college coach has removed his sport jacket and flung it to the floor. Passion is as high, or even higher, in the so-called amateur ranks as it is when people play for pay. One maneuver which to date has remained the exclusive property of the pros, however, is the tossing of the ball rack at an official. Thus far, the act was recorded as being done by both Indiana coach Bob ("Slick") Leonard and Cleveland coach Bill Fitch, each of whom drew heavy fines from their respective league commissioners.

The snipers are less obvious, but frequently far more cutting, than the screamers. Chicago's Motta, for example, cuts a dashing figure on the bench, as he sits there impeccably attired and elegantly coiffed. When calls upset him, he doesn't stomp, or even stride, to the midcourt line. On some occasions, he drops to a crouching position in front of his bench and assumes a pained look. That is as much as the public ever sees. What they don't know, however, is that Motta is carefully designing a plot to unnerve the officials once the ball comes downcourt. "Get that animal off our backs," he says softly but clearly and audibly to an official as soon as Dave Cowens gets a rebound for the Celtics. "That's right, protect the superstar," he says in the same sharp but muted tone when Walt Frazier goes to the foul line. Only someone sitting very close to him would hear him and realize that he is baiting the officials, but the officials are more than aware.

The intent of his early sniping, of course, is to turn the officials' attention toward things he wants them to see. If he can succeed in getting a loose ball foul called on Cowens in a key situation, for instance, and it's called because the official is subconsciously paying close attention to what Cowens is doing—because of Motta's constant taunts—then he has helped his team.

When a Heinsohn leaps up, curls his lips, waves his arms, and screams at an official at the top of his lungs, he is inviting the ultimate officiating weapon.

The tactic is all part of the game, and Motta is not the only one who does it. Holzman is a sniper, as is Bill Russell. The favorite cry of screamers and snipers alike remains the same as it has always been in the pro leagues: "Call 'em both ways, will ya?"

There comes a time in the life of every sniper when he finds that despite his helpful reminders things are still not going his way. It's then that he begins to get personal, and instead of "You're still protecting Hayward," the cry becomes "You never did have any guts." It is at this point, when innuendo replaces possible fact, that the official is more than likely to turn around, place his left hand in a vertical position and top it with his right hand in a horizontal position, forming a large "T." Translation: a technical foul and a $50 fine from the league office.

Technical fouls at the wrong time (in the final minute of a close game, for instance) can be disastrous. More than one coach has cost his team a victory by getting a mistimed technical. Any player, coach, or other team personnel, such as a trainer, who receives two technicals in one game is immediately ejected and must retire to the dressing room. Thus, coaches are generally more subdued after getting a first technical. Many fans, not to mention players on teams piloted by notorious accumulators of personal fouls, fervently hope that if a technical is forthcoming, it will come early in the game. The coach can then settle down and concentrate on coaching, and will be less likely to incur an additional and more costly technical in a later, more important portion of the game.

Technical fouls *can* be useful. When Red Auerbach coached the Celtics, he was known to deliberately get himself thrown out of ball games to arouse his team. "Lots of times," he admits, "we were flat and just couldn't get anything going.

So I'd pick a fight with Sid Borgia—or somebody, get myself a couple of technicals, and get thrown out of the game—just to see what would happen."

What usually happened was that the crowd would react loudly and violently to the treatment of their coach (Red reserved this tactic for home games) and start stomping and clapping. The team would pick up, run off 10 or 12 straight points, and be back in the ball game.

Auerbach, of course, was Auerbach, and there has never been another like him. During Heinsohn's sickness in November of 1974, he took over the team one night in Atlanta. It was the first time he had coached in an emergency capacity in five years. Early in the fourth period the club had fallen behind by 11 points, when suddenly Auerbach was involved in an incident with veteran referee Richie Powers, an old antagonist. He drew a first technical for his all-too-vivid description of a three-second call against the Celtics. Then he said to Powers, "You still have rabbit ears." The key word, obviously, was "still." "You're absolutely right," replied Powers, slapping him with a second technical. Red stomped off to the locker room.

The team responded with 10 points in the next 1:20 and went on to win the game on a last-second basket by John Havlicek, who had served as chairman of a committee that ran the club for the last eight minutes. Auerbach denied he had gotten himself thrown out deliberately, but it was hard to believe him. He had been seen in action too many times.

Another and perhaps the most important job of a coach in coaching a game is the proper use of his available personnel. His life would certainly be simpler if all players were Havliceks, Chamberlains, Russells, or Archibalds, capable of playing, in their respective primes, 45 to 48 minutes a night. Unfortunately, iron men are rare, and a

There isn't a professional coach who can sit through a game without saying something to the officials about the calls.

184

coach must face the reality that substitutions will be required on the basis of the rest factor alone.

Once substitutions have been initiated on both sides, the game often becomes a chessboard affair called "match-ups." Certain players on a given team are best suited to guard certain players on their opponent's. A coach must recognize the inequities that crop up and should be ready to exploit them. If a big guard like Frazier or Havlicek —when he is in the backcourt—finds himself matched with one of the smaller guards, it makes sense to take advantage of the size discrepancy and call plays that send the bigger man down low. If a coach has a big guard on the bench when his rival inserts a small guard, he should perhaps think about sending his big backcourtman in. It works conversely, too; a coach might believe a smaller man can cause more problems for a bigger man. Similar situations can occur when the power forwards are matched against the quick forwards.

In addition to the substitutions needed to rest people and take advantage of match-ups, a coach must think beyond the game at hand and consider his less experienced players. No coach wants to be known as a quitter, but there are times in the course of a season when he knows that, regardless of the score, his team is out of a game in the fourth period. The key is to know when. A team might be trailing by 13 points with six minutes to go and still be alive, but on another occasion, it might be as close as 10 with the same time left and have little chance of winning. In the latter instance, a coach is justified in pulling his veterans to try out some of his younger players, if only to give them experience. Though a coach's immediate goal is to win every game every night, he should realize the task is impossible. By developing a young player in whatever situation he can, he might have a more useful player at his disposal

during the playoffs. Injuries and foul trouble have cast strange players into key playoff roles, and those players who have had the most experience fare the best.

There are other situations in which the coach must think ahead. During the course of a season there are stretches where games pile up. Suppose, for example, the Knicks are in Oakland in the second game of a three-games-in-three-nights stretch on the west coast, and find themselves behind by 17 points with seven or eight minutes left to play. Holzman doesn't want to tire out his players any more than he has to; they have a game the next night in Seattle and a reasonably long plane ride to face. To have his team as fresh as it can be the next evening, he follows what is considered to be standard operating procedure in the professional ranks: he pulls his frontline players, accepts his loss to the Warriors, and starts thinking about the game against the Super Sonics.

Motivation is the key to success during the regular season. The schedule is so long and drawn out that the players find it extremely difficult to put forth their greatest efforts every night. This aspect of the pro game is hard for college coaches to accept when they come into the pros. They are used to a rah-rah spirit and a 26-game schedule in which the average college player performs to the best of his ability on every occasion. A pro schedule is over three times as long and, as any player on a good team knows, beyond that the mentally grinding pressure of the playoffs must be endured. Under such circumstances, coaching becomes a different proposition.

How, therefore, does a coach motivate his players? Is it by delivering a fervent oration before each game and at the half? Hardly. Basically it comes down to this: being able to demonstrate that the method he chooses to implement is a winning one. It was a football player, Bob Tucker,

Coaches generally can be grouped under two headings, screamers and snipers. Screamers are easily visible to the fans. The snipers are less obvious, but more cutting. Bill Russell is a sniper.

who summed it up best: "People talk about George Allen and what a motivator he is and that's a lot of baloney. Take Vince Lombardi. He treated them like dogs, but when the season was over they were spending playoff checks and wearing championship rings. The next year, when he again treated them like dogs, they didn't mind because they knew that if they did what he told them, they'd be champions again. Winning. That's what motivation is all about."

Whether a coach's basic nature is fatherly or tyrannical, whether he is a backslapper or a parsimonious distributor of compliments, whether he is steeped in technical knowledge or prefers to roll the basketball out on the floor and say, "Go to it, boys," doesn't really make any difference. People will play for him only if they believe in him.

The Celtics of old believed in Red Auerbach. Undoubtedly his greatest achievement—make that "their" greatest achievement—was not in winning all those playoff crowns. To do that they needed some luck to augment their skill. No, their crowning glory was in winning eight consecutive *regular season* titles from 1957 through 1965. Anyone can get up for the playoffs, but only men with pride and great character can arouse themselves, year after year, to go out and win the regular season when they know, given a minimum of breaks, they'd eventually win the playoff title and, along with it, the designation of world champions.

That's why Auerbach deserves full credit. Having talented players is one thing, but manipulating them is another. He had to keep them from becoming complacent, and he did it in a number of ways, not the least of which was his demand that they report to training camp ready to play and not in drastic need of a body overhaul. He drilled into them the concept of getting off to a great start, of leading the field by 10 games in January and putting the pressure on others to catch up.

"They knew that if they did what he told them, they'd be champions again. Winning. That's what motivation is about."

189

He worked them extremely hard during training camp, assuring them, one and all, that they were not important in his eyes. He also made sure that everything they did was as a team.

Modern athletes, however, are primarily self-motivating. Only the rarest of coaches can manipulate emotions, and then only with certain players.

NBA coaches are either ex-pros or college-trained, though basically there exists a two-to-one ratio in favor of ex-players. The fact is that through the 1973–74 season, not one of the collegiately trained coaches working in the NBA had yet won a championship. The most successful ABA coach, in terms of championships won, has been Indiana's Bob Leonard, an ex-NBA player. Half of the ten coaches who began the 1974–75 season in the ABA were ex-pros, with Virginia's Al Bianchi being widely regarded as the man who gets the most out of not enough.

Though the ex-pros have dominated the championships in both leagues, the collegians have brought to the league a high level of application and technical expertise. In some cases, the college coaches have failed because of their inability to control professionals off the court, being used to more submissive young college men. In other cases, they didn't get off to fast starts and were victims of a quick hook from above. Just as a player must learn that being able to adjust to changing situations is the key to success, so must coaches learn to bend a bit.

The sheer length of the season is a new ex-

The professional basketball coaching fraternity encompasses a wide range of people who are generally less stereotyped than their counterparts in other sports.

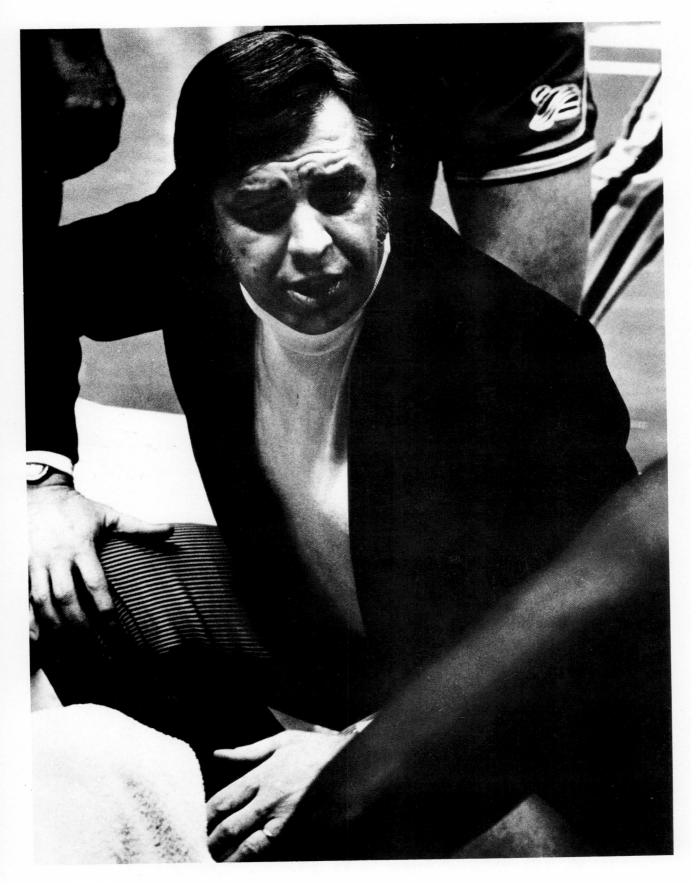

perience for rookie players and coaches alike. Fans and writers often can't understand why a great player or even a whole team falls into a dry spell in the second half of the season, playing several games in a stretch in which they bear no resemblance to the smooth-functioning machine of October, November, December, and January. Tom Heinsohn can explain it because he has lived through it, as both a player and a coach.

"Along about February," he explains, "it's rubber room time. You get sick of looking at each other, you object to each other's smelly feet, or some other silly thing. It's just a phase that comes and goes, and you have to understand it to be able to cope with it."

If there is one thing that all coaches have in common it's a will to win. Bill Fitch had always been a winner at his prior stops, which included Coe College, North Dakota University, and the University of Minnesota. When he took over the expansion Cleveland Cavaliers in 1970, he was realistic, but hopeful. His team stumbled through a 15–67 season that severely tested his resilience and brought out one of his great redeeming virtues, his sense of humor. It wasn't until the 1974–75 season that his team attained respectability and he was able to recall that old winning feeling. "I'm the world's worst loser," he said. "Ask anybody who has ever played anything with me, whether it was checkers or cards or one-on-one."

And if he is the world's worst loser, where does that leave Milwaukee's Larry Costello, who seemingly thinks about basketball 16 hours a day, always dreaming up new ways to get the ball in to Kareem Abdul-Jabbar? This is the man who allegedly went with a party to New York's Copacabana in 1971 to celebrate his team's playoff triumph and wound up diagramming plays on a napkin. Costello, with his dedication and zeal, is perhaps the only NBA coach in recent years to

approach the level of the average football coach. When Abdul-Jabbar missed the first month of the 1974–75 season because of a broken hand and an eye injury, the Bucks lost 13 of their first 14 games and Costello sank into complete and utter despair. "I've tried everything," he wailed after his team held the Celtics to seven points in the first period of a game and wound up losing. "I just don't know what to do."

Motta is another very hard loser. He sees his players as latter-day Don Quixotes surging at windmills. After a particularly tough loss he appears ready to jump off the top of the Wrigley Building, but not before questioning the intelligence and character of his players, the referees, and especially himself.

One of the real gentlemen in the game is Gene Shue, lately of Philadelphia, but for several years the successful coach of the electrifying Baltimore Bullets. Many coaches will search out and locate innumerable alibis for a loss, ranging from the inadequacy of the officiating to the stupidity of the players to the time zone change to the height of the baskets to the whim of fate. Not Shue. He offers no alibi, despite all the chances he has had in his coaching career to attribute a loss to one of the innumerable injuries that have plagued his teams. He even handles his beefs with officials differently than most, and he doesn't get many technical fouls. When he really had something to say one year, he made his remarks in public and wound up paying a costly fine to league commissioner Walter Kennedy. Attempting to find a past player of Shue's who dislikes him is not easy either.

The professional basketball coaching fraternity encompasses a wide range of people who are generally less stereotyped than their counterparts in other sports. It is doubtful if football or hockey can claim a man as cultured as Heinsohn,

A ball game, with all its
excitement and tension,
is potentially dangerous, yet
they seem to thrive on it.

who, despite his bulldog countenance, North Jersey dockhand accent, and gruff manner during a game, is an amateur painter and art connoisseur. Probably no other sport has a man like Cotton Fitzsimmons, who once spent a summer in Houston living in the ghetto to familiarize himself with blacks. Certainly no football team is run by more of a man's man than Ray Scott, the Detroit coach who when he isn't watching one of his old fight films is instilling some defense and on-court discipline into a ball club that lacked both attributes for years.

For these men, and for all the diverse personalities who coach in both leagues, running a ball club offers a challenge that few other endeavors could. A ball game, with all its excitement and tension, is potentially dangerous, yet they seem to thrive on it. Whether they are like Heinsohn, who was considered the unlikeliest of all coaching candidates from Auerbach's great Celtic teams of the late fifties and early sixties, or like Paul Johnson (Motta's protégé), who claims he knew at age 12 that he wanted to coach, they are dedicated to the game and possess an emotional intensity and physical drive that far transcends that of the average individual.

The championship, of course, is the ultimate goal. Even if, like Heinsohn or Bill Sharman (Los Angeles' excellent coach, and the only man to date who ever won championships in three different professional leagues—the ABL, ABA, and NBA), they have played on a championship team, they find that no thrill exceeds that of coaching the title winners. "There is no comparison," Heinsohn said after his Celtics defeated the Bucks in 1974. "When you're a player, you only have to prepare yourself. A coach has to worry about twelve men, and there is a greater feeling of accomplishment for him."

"When you're a player, you only have to prepare yourself. A coach has to worry about twelve men, and there's a great feeling of accomplishment."

194

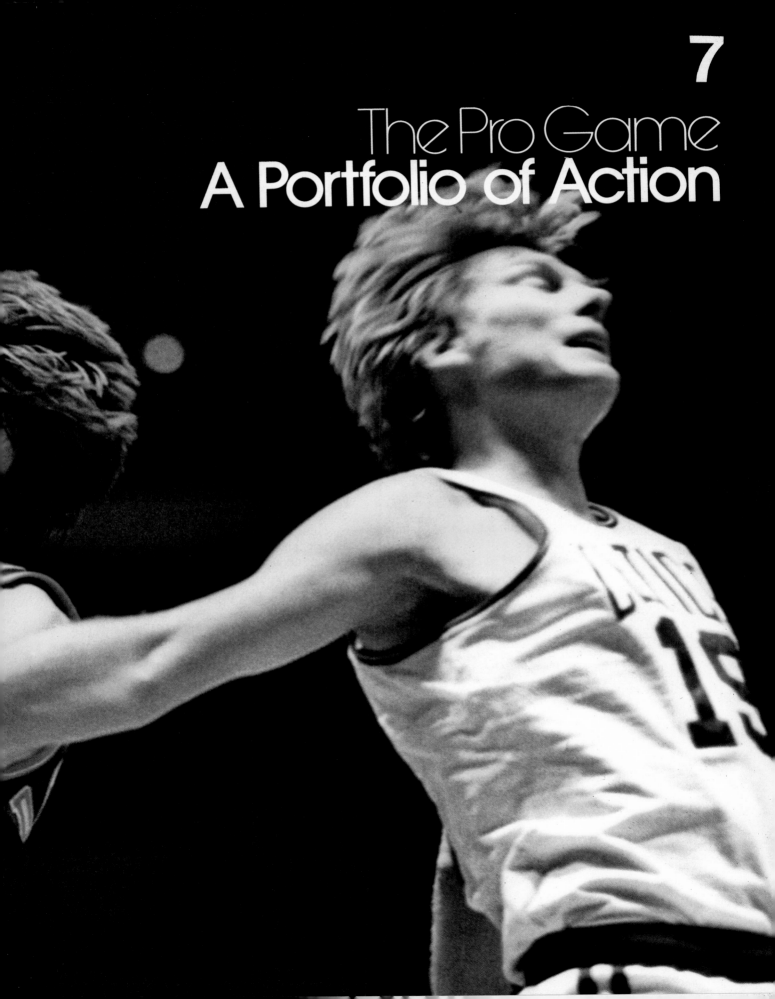

7

The Pro Game
A Portfolio of Action

There is, in basketball, an opportunity to express even that one great feeling of exultation—the basketball comeback. Thanks to the 24-second clock (recently being used also in the ABA), comebacks are more plentiful in professional basketball. It is hard to put a team completely out of a game, for the players know that at least they will receive the ball every 24 seconds. Comebacks have a snowballing effect. A couple of routine baskets reduce, say, an 18-point deficit to 14. A 3-point play and a steal suddenly cut it to 9, and now the game has taken on new meaning. If it's the home team executing the comeback, the crowd starts to make noise, and then, if the game follows the typical pattern, the officials get into the act, viewing the other team's actions more sternly than before. They keep coming and coming until finally somebody makes a superb play to put them ahead, possibly for the first time in the game. Any basketball fan knows what a euphoric feeling that moment gives.

There are few sports thrills comparable to that which is generated by a down-to-the-wire professional game, with two great teams swapping baskets and making good use of every available second. The rules of the game are geared to help the team coming up from behind. The clock stops automatically every time the ball drops through the hoop in the last two minutes, and teams calling a time out from out of bounds get the ball at

midcourt. Leads can change hands five or six times in the last minute in NBA games, and it's even more exciting in the ABA with its three-point field goal.

There is a feeling of involvement and enthusiasm generated by a basketball game that is exceeded by no other team sport. DeBusschere, who also played professional baseball with the Chicago White Sox, says, "I found basketball more competitive. I was a pitcher, so I worked once every four days. The rest of the time I chewed tobacco and played "Password" in the bullpen, and that's not too terribly exciting. Basketball was exciting." Now he watches games in a three-way bind. He is part ABA commissioner, part ex-player, and part fan. "I see myself as a combination of all three," he says. "I enjoy the game. It's impossible not to become excited over what people do. I appreciate the good things people do on the floor."

He also can readily appreciate the special skills of the great players. Though he had not been overly gifted himself, he was able to sustain his career through hard work. "I'm envious when I see the way some guys handle the ball, or the speed they have. I always wanted to have speed. It must be great to be able to run full speed, then stop quick and go up for a jumper like a Havlicek or a West could."

The pleasure inherent in watching huge, graceful men like Abdul-Jabbar and Lanier and clever little men like Archibald and Calvin Murphy, as well as Julius Erving, with his singular genius, would be enough to justify watching basketball strictly from an aesthetic point of view. But when a game combines these special thrills with a spirit of emotional involvement on the part of the whole team, it qualifies as a unique spectator experience.

Basketball is, quite simply, a beautiful game.

Each player must be part acrobat. Even when there is no way to get from here to there, when there is simply no path to the basket, enterprising players find a way to score.

**Defense should begin before
the man receives the ball . . .**

**. . . because after he gets it
it may be too late.**

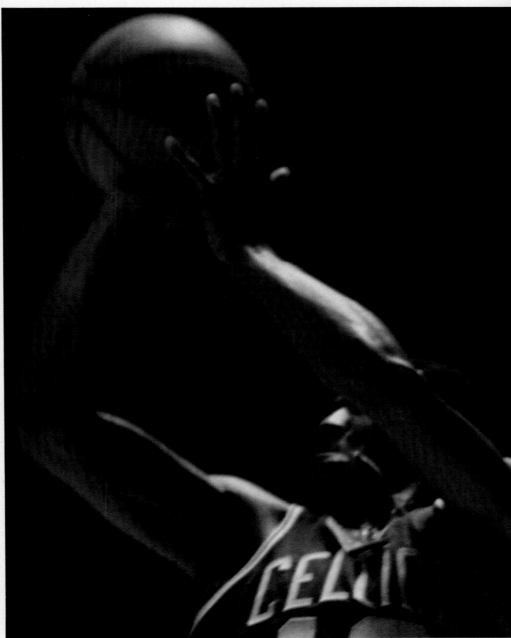

Team defense means "helping out." With three Nets converging on him, Byron Beck should be thinking about finding an open man. He will have to find one quickly.

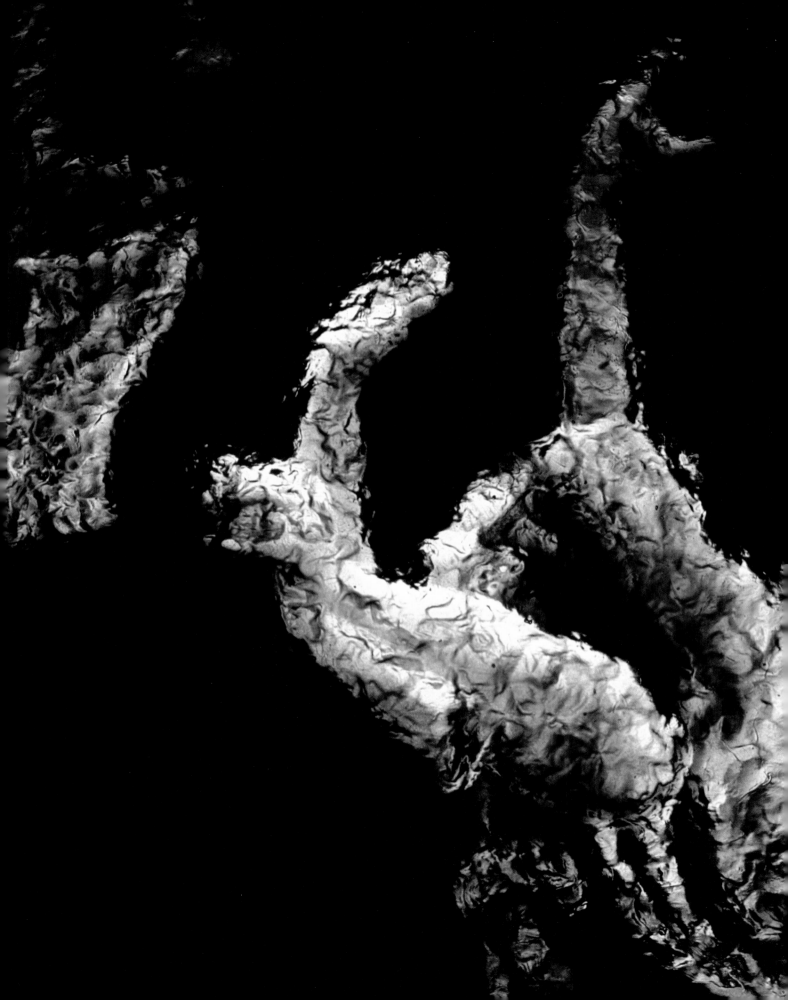

Hard work produces shots for the great offensive players. Through constant movement, they often seem only fleeting impressions to their opponents.

Though other athletes marvel at their conditioning and proclaim basketball players the best physical animals of all, even the best need an occasional rest.

Dr. J.'s ominous presence can scare any man.
Intimidation is a real part of the game.

Driving the baseline seemed a good idea
at the time to Jim McMillian. He forgot he
was messin' around on Dave Cowens' turf.

Feet spread, hands extended,
eyes fixed on the opponent—
that's the textbook way
to play defense.
There's also the more
physical approach.

Against the "sky hook," however,
there is no known defense.

Only the ignorant call it a noncontact sport.
Physical danger can come from friends . . .

. . . or foes.

It takes heart for a skinny guy to join
in the rebound battle.

Rebounding is the product of
timing, muscling, leaping, and
most of all, will power.

217

Sometimes it seems as though
men float to the basket.

No maneuver in sports brings the crowd
to its feet more readily than the . . .

STUFF!

Intense players are safety hazards
to press table occupants. Saving
a loose ball might mean the deciding
basket in a one-point game.

**There is danger when a
slender guard is hit from behind by a
250-pound center. But most players are agile
enough to avoid seemingly certain collisions.**

Emotions are not hidden behind masks, nor are the
players too far away to see. This is the most human
of team sports, the players the most identifiable.
As John Mengelt advances, trying to find
an opening, the crowd can think along with him.

A suitable grimace, accompanied by a decent groan, might produce the desired offensive foul.

In the final analysis, all the running, crashing, and plotting is for but one purpose—to put the ball into the basket.

The sight of large men performing graceful movements has always fascinated members of the artistic community. The additional fact that 10 gigantic (to the average person they are most certainly gigantic) men function within the confines of a court 94 feet long and 50 feet wide provides an added dimension. Great basketball players bring to the game a high degree of body control, which allows them to elude contact that would be inevitable for the less-gifted athlete.

Basketball has been likened to ballet. Indeed, there are soaring leaps and pirouettes and, especially when viewed from above, breathtaking moments of spectacular and exquisite artistry. To have seen Cousy feed a blind pass over his shoulder to Heinsohn, who would immediately feed underneath to Russell for a stuff, was to see the game in its most artistic form. To see the majestic sweeping hook of Kareem Abdul-Jabbar is to watch swan-like grace.

8

Prisoners of the Road
Behind the Scenes

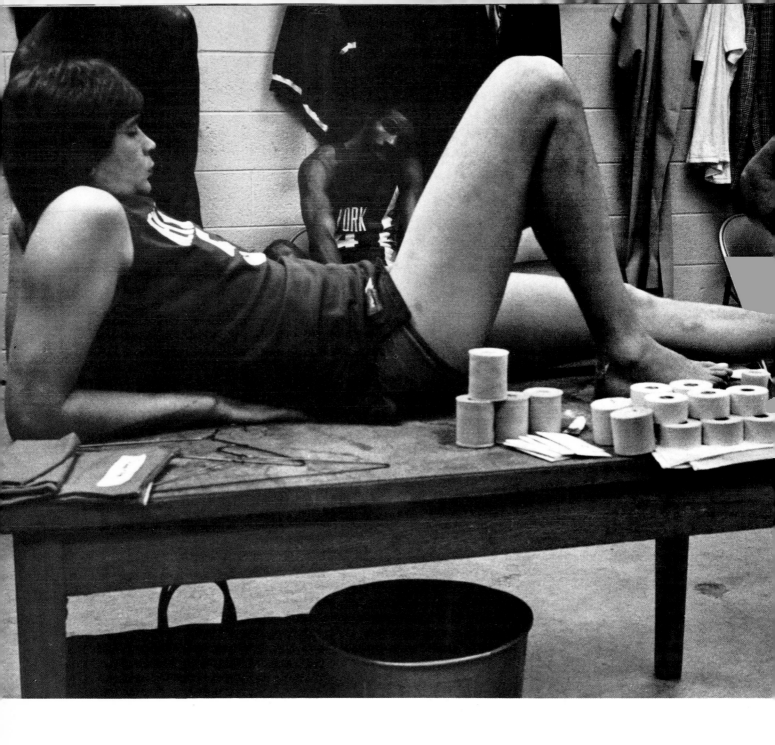

A trainer's supplies now extend far beyond
the basic aspirin, rubbing alcohol, and Band-Aids.
He is in charge of expensive equipment.

240

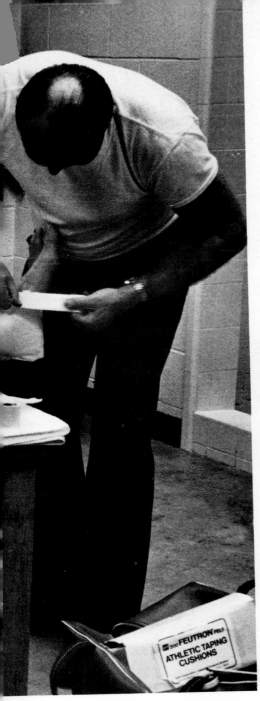

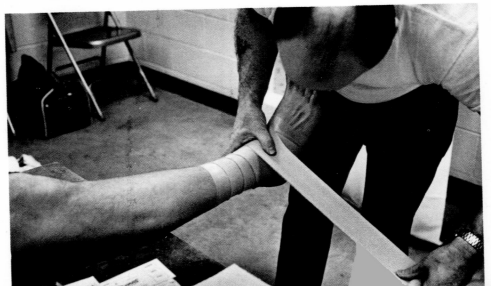

241

244

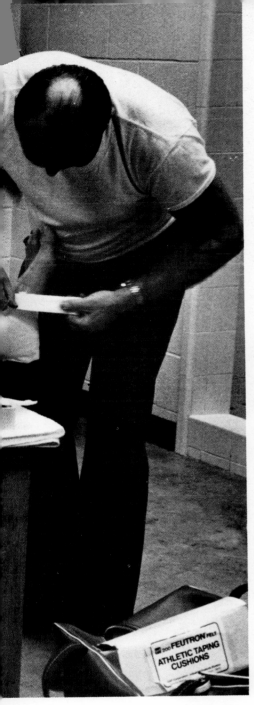

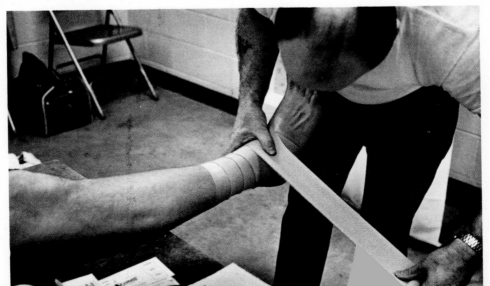

241

is also the team's traveling secretary. If he knows his way around the "Airline Guide" and has made proper contacts in the airline industry, he can often extricate his team from a bad travel situation.

The trainer shares the team's joys and sorrows, but all too often he winds up as the coach's scapegoat when something goes wrong. And he, too, finds—as does the athlete—that being on the road loses its mystique quickly. With very few exceptions, most players would prefer to play 80 percent of their games at home—as long as they could choose where to play the other 20 percent.

Modern life in pro basketball has one great advantage over its predecessor. The arenas are not like they used to be, and that is a very good thing. For a variety of reasons, going on the road used to mean conceding a loss. Old NBA auditoriums, such as the ones in Ft. Wayne, Syracuse, Rochester, Minneapolis, and St. Louis—not to mention the famed Philadelphia Convention Hall—could all be classified as "pits," around which howling mobs hovered in wait of unsuspecting basketball teams from the outside world. There was always an aura of violence and aggressiveness hanging over those places, and frequently there really was trouble. The crowds, being closer to the court, seemed to frighten officials more than modern crowds do. Good teams considered it a disgrace to lose at home, and clubs such as Minneapolis and Rochester didn't very often.

Some of the records at home were unbelievable. Minneapolis was 26–3, 30–1, 29–3, 21–5, 24–2, and 21–4 on its home floor from 1948–49 through 1953–54. Rochester, meanwhile, was going 24–5, 33–1, 29–5, 28–5, 24–8, and 18–10 in the same span.

Gradually the cramped, old arenas and their leather-lunged, workingman-type followers were

After the game the players have either a bus or cabs waiting for them and they go back to the hotel. When they arrive at the next destination they take a bus or cabs to the hotel— and so the process is repeated.

phased out, mainly because the league abandoned the cities they served. Rochester moved to Cincinnati and then to Kansas City. Ft. Wayne moved to Detroit. Syracuse moved to Philadelphia. Minneapolis moved to Los Angeles. The new cities had bigger, less intimate arenas and the atmosphere became much less combative and much more competitive.

This is not to say that some places are not more difficult to play in than others, even today. Undoubtedly, teams would prefer to keep their visits to Madison Square Garden to a minimum. Many teams wish that Phoenix would sink back into the desert. The "Valley of the Sun" does not rank high on the league's list of favorite tourist spots. The city itself might, but the Veterans Memorial Coliseum, where the Phoenix wolves sit, doesn't.

The Suns fans are considered to be among the league's more hostile. They are rabid and incredibly partisan. They love to get on the visiting team, and they don't treat officials with utmost respect either. Any call, no matter how obvious or flagrant, that goes against the Suns is bad. Little allowance is made for the Suns' culpability in any case. It makes for a strange, but interesting, experience. The funny part is that most people have a sort of "Retirement City" image of Phoenix, when in reality the town is more like the last frontier. Cowboy hats, boots, and string ties abound, lending a colorful flavor to a game played there.

Veterans Memorial Coliseum is also one of the two NBA arenas where the dressing room has a show biz motif, with makeup-type lights placed in the tables. The Bucks have a similar arrangement in their Milwaukee Arena dressing room.

Fortunately for visiting teams, the Suns have never consistently packed in crowds over ten thousand strong. They have had a steady clientele of from seven to eight thousand, which makes more than enough noise. But if the Suns ever do get those ten-thousand-plus crowds, the visiting clubs will really have something to worry about.

The northwest franchises of Portland and Seattle have also distinguished themselves with tough, aggressive, highly vocal, and extremely partisan crowds, perhaps because for the first several years of their existence they, like Phoenix, were the only major league show in town. It seems that when a city has only one major professional sports team, it lavishes upon that team—or at least its adherents do—an affection and protectiveness that is part high schoolish, and is part mother eagle.

Games in the Seattle Center Coliseum, a beautiful building constructed for Seattle's World's Fair, are notable for two reasons. The first is that the horn used is capable of awakening slumbering residents in Nairobi, Kenya, and the second is that it sometimes seems as though the dressing rooms in the building are located in downtown Tucumcari, New Mexico.

Seattle fans are amazing. They have turned out in increasingly greater numbers despite the severe economic slump that fell on their city long before it hit the rest of the nation. Seattle was known to be largely a one-economy town, supported primarily by the aircraft industry. When defense cutbacks began in the late sixties and early seventies, disaster was predicted for the Super Sonics. Instead, the franchise, surviving some bad on-court problems, has proved to be one of the league's best.

Both the Seattle Center Coliseum and the Portland Memorial Coliseum are typical of the sparkling arenas in which professional basketball is played today.

Probably no team appreciates what it means to have a good facility more than the New York

Modern life in pro basketball has one great advantage over its predecessor. The arenas are not like they used to be.

Nets. They used to play in a fascinating structure sadistically named the "Island Gardens" in Hempstead, Long Island. Their dressing room, though a joke, was far superior to that of the visiting players, who more often than not dressed at their hotel rather than use it. The arena looked like a miniature airplane hangar, and it was marvelously lopsided. Now the Nets play in the beautiful Nassau Coliseum in Uniondale, Long Island.

With the temporary exception of New Orleans, which was forced to play in the ancient Municipal Auditorium in the first half of its first NBA season, the only teams in the NBA still playing in old arenas are Boston and Chicago. The league has come a long way if those two places are the worst the league has to offer, because both are blessed with their own peculiar charm.

The Boston Garden has a beautiful parquet floor—the only one of its kind in basketball—and awesome rows of championship flags and retired numbers suspended from its roof. The dressing rooms, once likened to the Black Hole of Calcutta, have been renovated and offer no threat to anyone's health.

Chicago Stadium does have a problem with its visiting team dressing rooms; management's idea of comfort seems to be a couple of park benches. The highlight of the stadium is an immense organ, and the acoustics there are phenomenal. A crowd of eight or ten thousand whooping it up for the Bulls, backed by that organ, makes an unbelievable roar.

The only acoustics to rival Chicago Stadium's are those in Madison Square Garden. Knick fans can make a lot of noise, and they often unnerve their rivals while inspiring the Knicks. It seems strange that noise can be interpreted as "pro" or "anti," depending on when or why the fans are yelling, despite the fact that it sounds exactly the same to both teams on the court. In New York, the

In addition to coffee shops, players reluctantly discover they must spend a lot of time in airports, which are mostly Machiavellian inventions.

fans are capable of generating both types of noise.

The crowd is only one factor in determining the scope of a team's homecourt advantage. There are clear differences, for example, in lighting (Portland's seems somehow subdued), tightness of rims, and playing surface. It was no secret that the old Madison Square Garden rims were very loose, or "soft." In fact, they were so loose, and so good for shooters (balls could hit the rim reasonably hard and wind up having been deadened enough to drop into the basket), that they earned the nickname of "sewers."

The Boston Garden possessed a set of rims second in shooting aid only to those in New York. But the Celtics purchased brand new rims prior to the start of the 1974–75 season, and thus was another league idiosyncrasy relegated to memory.

As long as the Houston Rockets played in the University of Houston's Hofheinz Pavilion, they should have enjoyed a handsome homecourt advantage, inasmuch as theirs was the only home floor not made out of wood. They played on a Tartan surface, which definitely requires some adjustments before a player can feel completely comfortable on it. When the Atlanta Hawks played their home games at Alexander Coliseum, the Georgia Tech field house, there were numerous complaints about the hardness of that particular floor, which was likened to playing on the Pennsylvania Turnpike.

One more spot that will not be missed is the late, but hardly lamented, Cleveland Arena. The basic problem with that seedy structure had been the inside temperature, which rarely seemed to reach even the level of the Cavaliers' first-half scoring totals. The arena's locker rooms will be mourned least of all, however, except by those peculiar players who, while showering, enjoyed the zesty change of water temperature from arctic blast to tropical tingle when somebody flushed a toilet. The Cavaliers' move in 1974 to a new suburban palace was warmly received by the players.

For real tales of deprivation an ABA original would have to be described. However, like its big brother, the ABA is rapidly shedding its dependence on outmoded arenas.

One aspect of sports that never becomes outmoded is the way players relate to one another, and that includes the behavior witnessed in Little League (or its basketball, football, or hockey equivalent) right up to and through the professional ranks. Athletes have a way of speaking, thinking, and acting that, having been so thoroughly ingrained, becomes natural for them.

To be an athlete one must have a sense of humor, be a kidder. Players have an incessant need to stay loose, to relax from the tension they find themselves in daily. The pressure to produce constantly in order to remain employed could obliterate every other aspect of a man's life if he'd let it. Multiply that tension by the interaction of 12 men, as on a professional basketball team, and the situation could be deadly were not humor used as a release.

The important thing though is how a player kids. The low blow must be avoided. Cutting remarks about a man's wife or girl friend or his

A player must first, however, survive the initial plane ride. Like it or not, they still must fly over a hundred thousand miles a year.

Many people envision a wild and exciting
run of coast-to-coast parties. The player would
like to know how he missed the orgy.

children are taboo. A man may be kidded about his playing style. For example, a man who shoots a great deal should expect to hear about it—kiddingly. But he most likely will not hear about a bad shot he took that cost his team a game. If he does, and if he hears it more than once, that particular team has a problem.

Basketball players, being in such a small number as a team, are thrown together most intimately when they travel for a season. They are generally housed two to a room, and go in cabs, buses, and airplanes together. They sit around together in the locker room before every practice and every game. Thus it is important that they get along with each other. More than one team has traced its on-court troubles to off-court hassling.

Ideally, of course, team members are genuinely friendly to one another. Gene Conley, who pitched in the major leagues in addition to playing for both the Celtics and New York Knicks, sums up what it was like for the Celtics of his day: "When we went on a road trip, it was like the family packing up and going off on a vacation."

Players don't necessarily have to be buddy-buddy. But they must be able to get along. A recent example was the championship Knicks team of the early seventies. They roomed together and ate together and played some fantastic ball together while on the road, but when they got back to New York they ran off in 12 different directions and rarely, if ever, socialized. None of them, apparently, saw the others as people he cared to share his leisure time with. But when they had to live and work together, they were able to. They were a very mature group of men, for there is little chance that no flare-ups occurred. Whatever problems the Knicks did have, they overcame.

Movies and television constitute the only entertainment for most of the players on the road. Many people envision a wild and exciting run of coast-to-coast parties with ample centerfold girls in attendance. If this is the case, the professional player would like to know how he managed to miss "the orgy." True, the ever-present groupies do exist, but most of them are harmless, their prime aim being to fill their autograph books.

More often than not, a player on the road has the distinct impression that he spends the greater part of every day waiting to go to the arena. Most teams request that their players arrive about an hour and a half before the game, but the Celtics, for one, deliver their players to the arena two hours before. Tom Heinsohn's policy has always been to close the locker room to press and assorted team personnel 45 minutes before the start of the game in order to conduct his pregame meeting. This gives his players at least an hour and a quarter to get taped, dressed, and go out and shoot a few baskets if there is no preliminary game. It also allows the individual player time to think about his opponents, to concentrate on and get mentally prepared for the game.

After the game the players have either a bus or cabs waiting for them and they go back to the hotel. Most players eat a good-sized dinner around three or four o'clock so they are hungry after a seven-thirty or eight o'clock game. Some might go out for a few beers before going to bed.

The next morning, players are awakened by hotel wakeups half an hour before the bus or cabs come to take them to the airport. Most players eat breakfast at the airport coffee shop, or possibly on the plane—although it is generally the worst meal the airline industry offers—and, if they have gotten up particularly early, they spend the morning sleeping en route.

When they arrive at the next destination, they take a bus or cabs to the hotel, and so the process is repeated.

Being on the road loses its mystique quickly. With very few exceptions, most players would prefer to play 80 percent of their games at home.

Player Identifications

front cover Dave Robisch, Julius Erving

back cover Earl Monroe, John Havlicek

2–3 John Mengelt, Fred Boyd

4–5 Walt Frazier

6–7 Phil Chenier

8–9 Willis Reed

11 James Naismith

14 Hank Luisetti

15 Sweetwater Clifton, George Mikan

18 Sam Jones, Matt Goukas

19 Tom Heinsohn, Bob Cousy, Slater Martin, Jim Loscutoff, Ed Macauley, Bill Sharman

21 Bob Cousy, Bill Russell, Guy Rodgers

22 Bill Russell, Wilt Chamberlain, John Havlicek, Hal Greer

25 left: Wilt Chamberlain; right: Wilt Chamberlain, Bill Russell

26 Willis Reed, Bill Russell

27 Bill Bradley

29 Jerry Lucas, Dave Cowens

30 Nate Hawthorne, Walt Frazier, Happy Hairston

31 Dean Meminger, Jerry West

32 Elvin Hayes, Tom Kozelko

33 Phil Jackson, Walt Frazier, Elvin Hayes

35 Wes Unseld, Dennis Awtrey, Billy Cunningham

36 Kevin Porter, Earl Monroe

37 top: Earl Monroe, Wes Unseld; bottom: Phil Chenier

39 Dancing Harry

43 Earl Monroe, Oscar Robertson

44 Ernie DiGregorio, Jim Cleamons

45 left: Ernie DiGregorio; right: Bob McAdoo, Ernie DiGregorio

46 Dave Cowens, John Gianelli

48 Kareem Abdul-Jabbar, LaRue Martin

49 Kareem Abdul-Jabbar

51 Bill Walton

52 John Gianelli, John Havlicek

53 John Havlicek, Jim McMillian, Bob McAdoo

56–57 Mendy Rudolph

58 Richie Powers

59 Tom Van Arsdale

60 Dick Van Arsdale, Randy Smith

61 Richie Powers

62 Billy Paultz, Mike Gale, Charlie Edge, George McGinnis

63 top: John Gianelli, Billy Oakes, Elvin Hayes, Walt Frazier; bottom: Mendy Rudolph

64 Julius Erving, Wendell Ladner, Bruce Seals, Ron Boone

65 Larry Kenon, Mel Daniels

66 Phil Jackson, Gar Heard

68 Jim Capers

69 left: Mendy Rudolph; right: Billy Oakes

70 top: Mike Gale, George McGinnis, Larry Kenon; bottom: Jimmy Clark, Mike Gale, Artis Gilmore

71 Mendy Rudolph

72 Happy Hairston, Bob McAdoo

74 Mendy Rudolph, Billy Oakes

76–77 Leroy Ellis, Elvin Hayes

78 Billy Oakes

80 Mike Riordan, Steve Mix, Elvin Hayes

82 Don Murphy

83 Hawthorne Wingo, Mendy Rudolph, Billy Oakes

84 Mendy Rudolph

87 Mendy Rudolph

88–89 John Gianelli, Elmore Smith

90 Artis Gilmore

91 John Gianelli, Dave Cowens

93 Russell Lee, Jon McGlocklin, Kareem Abdul-Jabbar, Larry Costello, Jack McKinney

94 left: Bill Walton, Kareem Abdul-Jabbar, Kevin Restani; right: John Gianelli, Elmore Smith

97 Dave Cowens, Wilt Chamberlain

99 Leroy Ellis, Elvin Hayes

100 Billy Paultz

103 top: Bob Lanier; bottom: Artis Gilmore, Billy Paultz

104 Artis Gilmore, Ron Thomas

105 Barry Clemens, John Gianelli

106 LaRue Martin, Kareem Abdul-Jabbar

108 John Gianelli

109 Swen Nater, Willie Sojourner

112 Kareem Abdul-Jabbar, Don Murphy, Bill Walton

254

113 Dave Cowens
114 Billy Paultz, Artis Gilmore
115 Kareem Abdul-Jabbar
116–117 Julius Erving
118 Tom Van Arsdale
119 Larry Kenon, Dan Issel
120–121 Julius Erving, Dan Issel
122 Rick Barry
123 Dan Issel
124 Don Nelson, Dave DeBusschere
125 top: Jim McMillian, John Havlicek; bottom: Bob Netolicky
126 Julius Erving, George McGinnis
128 Mike Jackson
129 Tom Van Arsdale
131 Julius Erving, Swen Nater
132 Bill Bradley, Barry Clemens
133 Wilbert Jones, Gerald Govan
134 top: Bill Keller, Mike Gale, Julius Erving, George McGinnis, Larry Kenon; bottom: Bob Dandridge, Chet Walker
135 George Trapp, Steve Mix
136–137 Jim Price, Paul Silas
138 Rick Mount
139 Jo Jo White, Wes Unseld
140 left: John Williamson; right: Walt Frazier, Don Chaney
141 Austin Carr, Randy Smith
142 Ralph Simpson
144 Henry Bibby
147 Phil Chenier
148 top: Jo Jo White; bottom: Pete Maravich
149 Steve Mix, Tom Kozelko, Mike Riordan
150 Tom Van Arsdale, Mike Riordan
151 Larry Steele, Mickey Davis
152 left: Willie Norwood; right: Dave Bing, Norm Van Lier
153 Gary Melchionni
155 Walt Frazier, Don Chaney, Jo Jo White, Dean Meminger, Dave Cowens
157 Pete Maravich, Dennis Bell
158 Butch Beard
160 Butch Beard
161 Slick Watts, Gar Heard
162 Jimmy Walker
163 Dave Bing
164 Ernie DiGregorio, Bob McAdoo
165 left: Jimmy Jones, Bill Melchionni; right: Pete Maravich, Earl Monroe, George Trapp
166–167 Wilt Chamberlain
168 John Gianelli, Nate Hawthorne, Connie Hawkins
169 Joe Mullaney
170 Steve Mix, George Trapp, Don Adams, Larry Jones
171 Paul Silas, Dave Cowens, Jo Jo White, Don Nelson
172 Dave Bing, Tom Van Arsdale, Don Adams
175 Mike Gale, George Carter, Billy Paultz, Julius Erving
178 Ronnie Robinson, Joe Mullaney, Roy Ebron, Zelmo Beaty
179 Tom Heinsohn, Jake O'Donnell, John Havlicek
183 Tom Heinsohn
185 John MacLeod, Denny Price
186 Bill Russell
188 Gerald Govan, Wil Robinson, Glen Combs
189 Bill Bradley, Connie Hawkins, Elmore Smith
190 left: Alex Hannum; right: Kevin Loughery
191 Bill Van Breda Kolff
192 Bill Keller
193 top: Stew Johnson, Jim O'Brien, Louie Dampier
194 top: Babe McCarthy; bottom: Al Bianchi
195 Red Holzman
196–197 Terry Driscoll, Don Nelson
200 Larry Kenon, George Gervin
201 Leroy Ellis, Steve Mix, Elvin Hayes
202 Bo Lamar, Mike Gale
203 Jim Barnett, Jesse Dark
204 Stu Lantz, Fred Carter
205 Jo Jo White
206–207 Julius Erving, Wendell Ladner, Mike Gale, Byron Beck
208 Dan Issel
209 John Havlicek
210 Dave Cowens, Jim McMillian
211 Larry Kenon, Bo Lamar, Julius Erving
212 top: Elvin Hayes, Fred Carter; bottom: Tom Van Arsdale, Jimmy Walker

255

213 Bill Walton, Kareem Abdul-Jabbar
214 Bill Bridges, Jack Marin, Bob McAdoo, Jim McMillian, Happy Hairston
215 Cincy Powell, Coby Dietrick, Eugene Kennedy
216 Jerry Lucas, Don Nelson
217 John Gianelli, Phil Jackson
218 Artis Gilmore, Bo Lamar, Caldwell Jones
219 Billy Paultz
221 George Carter
224 Pete Maravich
225 Lucius Allen, Dale Schlueter, Mickey Davis
226 George McGinnis
227 Bob Lanier
228 John Mengelt
229 Jim Eakins, John Williamson
231 Bob Lanier
235 Kareem Abdul-Jabbar

237 John Havlicek
238 Cincy Powell
240 Billy Paultz, Brian Taylor, Fritz Massman
241 top: Jay Bauer; bottom: Fritz Massman
242 Caldwell Jones, Louie Dampier
244 Billy Paultz, Larry Kenon, Al Skinner, John Williamson
246 bottom left: Julius Erving, Kevin Loughery; bottom right: Mike Gale, Ed Manning; top: Larry Kenon, Mike Gale, John Williamson
247 Julius Erving, Billy Paultz
248 Billy Paultz, Larry Kenon, Al Skinner
250 Bill Melchionni
251 top: Julius Erving, Al Skinner, Willie Sojourner; bottom: Julius Erving, Al Skinner
253 John Williamson